I CRY IN THE SHOWER

Loving Silas Living With Cancer

GLORIA MARTIN

PRESS

INTRODUCTION

S ilas Martin is my third child, my baby. He also was my largest born, a fact he loved to share. His first brain tumor diagnosis was before he was six years old. From that point forward, Silas lived with cancer. The last brain tumor changed both of our lives profoundly, and ultimately ended his.

I started out writing this book, intending to record the journey Silas and I traveled over the course of his last bout with brain cancer. I wanted to share the things we did right, and the mistakes along the way, in hopes of helping others living through similar circumstances. I soon realized I couldn't do that without showing the history, capturing many of the experiences funneling into that last year. I had to show how Silas lived with cancer.

This book is a sort of diary. Sometimes it was God loving Silas through me. Sometimes it was just me loving Silas as his Mom. Sometimes I loved Silas as his primary caregiver and advocate. Sometimes it was Silas showing me how to love, how to live.

Each entry page is identified.

The history is **Silas Living With Cancer**. With hope. With faith. With perseverance.

The journey of his last brain tumor is **Loving Silas**. (I often posted these as updates in Facebook.)

Then, the tide turned. Silas was sent home from the hospital on hospice. With numbered days, our friends and family took care of us so we could simply let go and love each other. So I could let go and let God show me it had been **God Loving Us** all along.

ACKNOWLEGEMENTS

I want to thank Sara Bubenik Theis, who took my facebook entries and made them readable. I posted so many entries in the heat of the emotional roller coaster that was my life for fourteen months as I cared for Silas. Sara has intuition beyond her editing skills. She helped me to say what I actually meant.

All glory to God for the abundant life with which I am blessed, His endless mercy and grace, and the absolute certainty I will one day see Silas in heaven.

Loving Silas

November 3, 2013

2:22 a.m. It's time to turn the clocks back for Daylight Savings Time. The dogs woke me up, so I may as well start now. Suddenly I hear Silas upstairs, vomiting, holding his head in pain. I think it must be a virus. I call our pediatrician anyway, since Silas has been a brain tumor patient over the course of nine years. Of course, the doctor advises going to the ER. It feels like we've done this a million times. It looks like we won't be in church come morning. A phone call or two, grab a bucket to go in the car, and we're off, praying aloud on the way.

"Zofran is our friend." I say, as they hook him up to IVs and take blood. We learned that fact when Silas was on chemotherapy years ago.

Silas is whisked off for a CT scan, and I start to feel uneasy. We were here months earlier, after Silas had a comical accident at school. His little bump on the head had also resulted in a CT scan. Everyone in Silas' realm knows the drill: anything to do with his head must be checked out thoroughly. What providence that particular CT scan was.

It seems like hours, but I know it isn't. The image is clear, especially when compared, side-by-side, with the image from months earlier. There is a distinct, round, mass. This is the moment I realize how vast is my medical knowledge–and how much I hate knowing so much. ER doctor has already consulted St. Louis Children's Hospital and called for transport. I am told to go home and pack, come back to give Silas a kiss, and leave for SLCH.

I have driven this route dozens (hundreds?) of times. Only this time, I feel like I am driving right into the eye of a hurricane. All of my training, all the experiences God has allowed over months and years, have prepared me for this exact time. Of all the people I phone on my drive, the most memorable is the call to Traci Reichman, with Leaps Of Love, because she says she will meet me at the ER on that end. I talk to God, a lot. I don't remember exactly what I say, but I remember my words are words of praise. The music I choose to listen to — and sing with — are songs of praise. I don't know what else to do but to praise God. I don't know anything for sure about Silas' condition. I don't yet realize the bottom has dropped out of my world. The thing I do know, I know with absolute certainty: God is still God, and we are His.

I don't have to understand the physical realm, yet.

Asking "Why?" isn't going to do anyone any good. The only thing which is real to me in these moments in the car, is God is. God was. God will always be.

"Though the mountains be shaken and the hills be removed, yet my unfailing love for you will not be shaken nor my covenant of peace be removed," says the Lord, who has compassion on you." (Isaiah 54:10)

Leaps of Love is a non-profit organization, assisting childhood cancer families, focusing on brain tumors and late-effects of their treatments. 907 Main St., Highland, IL 62249 Phone – 618.410.7212

Loving Silas

Conversation is an art, especially when it takes place in an emergency examination room. I never say what I actually want to say. I make small talk. I ask healthcare workers about their families. I try to get them to talk about themselves, under the guise of being considerate. In reality, I avoid voicing my fears. I avoid admitting I already know the results of the MRI before the neurosurgeon arrives. I won't go there, because nobody will humor me and let me start preparations until it's confirmed. I simply want to get busy. I want to start organizing our lives around this new bump in the road which is Silas' journey.

I have two feelings right now. I hate. I love. I hate we are here right now. I love that we have been here before.

I hate I know it's a brain tumor. I hate I have to tell my son remission is over. I hate cancer is once again eating away at his brain. I hate that Silas will have to have surgery. I hate he will have to have treatment beyond surgery. I hate that the course of Silas' life has once again been altered.

I love I know it's a brain tumor. I love I find strength in knowledge. I love that I know what to do. I love I have prayer chains to mobilize, prayer partners to call. I love I know God has directed us to the right hospital once again. I love I have been here before with Silas, and that he trusts me to know what to do.

When I receive the "official" results, I shed a few tears before they bring Silas back to the exam room. We'll be moving from emergency to an in-patient floor in a little while, and I talk with Silas about his new brain tumor. We debate whether the upcoming surgery will be his 3rd or 4th craniotomy, and whether Touch Team Dogs visit patients on the weekend. We pray.

We have been here before. We are not alone.

"Be strong and courageous. Do not be afraid or terrified because of them, for the LORD your God goes with you; he will never leave you nor forsake you." (Deuteronomy 31:6)

Loving Silas

November 4, 2013

Silas is settled into his room. He calls the television set on the long, expandable arm a "crane tv." With his vision impairment, having the television close to his face is a blessing.

Once the pain and anti-nausea medicines kicked in and all the tests were done, Child Life Services brought Silas a Nintendo DS with games. They finally let him eat about thirty-six hours after waking up sick in the middle of the night. That is a long time to ask someone who dearly loves food to go without eating. He's being closely monitored, even if he doesn't look sick. I brought a book I've been wanting to read and never got around to. I'm actually reading it.

Tomorrow I plan to go to an AA meeting on Lindell Avenue. It's only a few blocks from the hospital. A friend from home is here in St. Louis as caregiver for her grandson also hospitalized. We plan to meet there to support each other. I feel so loved and held by God. We have such a phenomenal church family, amazing support network, and Silas' school friends and staff, Camden Foundation, Leaps of Love. I can't list all of you surrounding us and holding us up. Thank you.

Camden Foundation, Inc. is a non-profit organization based in Ivesdale, Illinois. The organization's mission focus is to raise money for childhood cancer research, bring awareness and knowledge of childhood cancer to surrounding communities, and sponsor families affected by childhood cancer in Central Illinois. (217) 722-9388)

Silas Living with Cancer

Silas Paul Martin was born August 3, 1998. By six months, he was diagnosed with Neurofibromatosis Type 1, or NF1, a genetic disorder characterized by multiple cafe-au-lait spots and neurofibromas on or under the skin. Occasionally, tumors may develop in the brain, on cranial nerves, or on the spinal cord. About fifty percent of people with NF also have learning disabilities. People with NF1 often experience only mild symptoms, as is the case with Silas' father.

By nine months, it was determined Silas had some developmental delays. He was enrolled in an early intervention program, which included a specialist coming to the house to work with Silas. She also worked with me, to teach me how to teach my child. He needed help to learn the things my other two children had simply learned normally.

There was nothing "normal" about Silas. He was unique, one of a kind, amazing.

Loving Silas

November 6, 2013

I'm in waiting room number two, 6th floor surgery, with Silas' dad, Brock, Silas' grandmother who he calls "Nona", Silas' youth pastor, Scott Monette, and our pastor, Steve Higgs. At 8:30, the doctors said surgery would begin in an hour and a half. The actual surgery was estimated to take about four hours. Before taking him back, Silas said he wasn't scared. He gave me a big hug because he knows I am terrified.

I never say that aloud.

Several hours later...

Dr. Leonard is done with surgery. I learned a new term: Total Gross Resection. That means he got all of the tumor. All he can see. He thinks it is a high grade glioma, which means it already has started infiltrating the surrounding area. Silas will need aggressive treatment starting immediately. The look on Dr. Leonard's face is forever etched in my memory. I have seen this man after surgery before. Never have I seen him look so grim. I feel like I'm on an elevator which suddenly is plummeting to the ground floor. I cannot imagine facing this without faith in God, and the support of all of those He has placed in our lives.

Silas is in the Pediatric Intensive Care Unit, PICU, by the time we catch up with him. He has been in and out of consciousness, but is recovering from surgery quickly. In true Silas form, when he heard our youth pastor, Scott Monette, was here, Silas wanted to know if he could tell him a joke. He then promptly fell back asleep. Now he's sucking on mouth swabs, but clear liquids are on the horizon. He will move to 12th floor sometime tomorrow, barring complications.

Silas will have an MRI first thing tomorrow and, hopefully, we'll move to the 12th floor from PICU afterwards. The swelling is beginning and is expected to peak late tomorrow. He got a new bear and blanket from the PICU staff. I'm starting research on high grade hemorrhagic glioma. SLCH has an awesome resource center to assist with that tomorrow as well. I want to know as much as possible about the enemy as we prepare for battle. God has this. I know that for sure in this moment. I, absolutely, positively, 100% believe and know that.

Loving Silas

November 8, 2013

Silas is kicking surgery's butt. He wowed the staff in 2010 with quick recovery, but this is amazing. It is the second day after brain surgery and he's up. He took the IV Pole, complete with his stuffed My Little Pony on it, for a stroll down the hall. I've not heard it from a doctor yet, but I think he could go home Sunday. Prayer moves mountains.

November 9, 2013

We're going home. Only the third day after surgery! Silas will rest for a week to ten days and then, we're back here with the whole team. They will do surgery to put in a Port-A-Cath, after which we're into IV Chemotherapy for months. Please keep the prayers coming. We truly feel them. We see God's hand in the midst of this. We're gearing up for the next attack in this battle.

November 10, 2013

Silas' strength and determination are astounding.

Today is Sunday. I wasn't sure if Silas would feel like going to church, but he was certain. During church today, one of the worship songs started while the entire congregation was seated. Silas grabbed my hand and told me he just couldn't sit and praise God. Up he went, the only person in the entire church standing and worshiping, only four days after brain surgery. I crept up beside him, humbled by my child. Others soon followed suit. What faith Silas has. What a grateful heart.

Silas Living With Cancer

When Silas was three years old, I awoke to a phone call around five a.m., from the owner of a local grocery. "Mrs. Martin," he said, "I think I have one of your children here." Sure enough, Silas got up in the middle of the night, wearing a pull-up and t-shirt. He pulled on his little tennis shoes, and exited through our back door, leaving it wide open and light on.

He was headed to his babysitter's house, about a mile away. He wanted to watch a favorite movie with her. That desire is all that was on his mind. He knew the route. Fortunately, someone saw him before he reached the state highway.

We didn't know these terms then, but Silas' sleep-wake cycle, or circadian rhythm, was disturbed. He would be fully awake suddenly at night, or fall asleep unpredictably during the day. We thought it odd, and frustrating; but we simply put locks high up on the inside of doors to keep him inside the house while we slept, and tried administering melatonin at night.

Loving Silas

November 17, 2013

I look at Exodus 18, and my sermon notes. Silas just had surgery for a PNET tumor, his first brush with cancer in years. I know this is most likely terminal. Pastor Steve Higgs' words make a huge impact on me this day. "You need to know your limits. You are not God. God has no limits."

I am limited by how much I can do for the Kingdom. I am limited by time, for one. I need to remember most of all, I do not have, nor will I ever have, all the resources I need, to help in all the possible ways I see before me. Alone, I do not have them, but as a body, we have the resources, if we are corporately relying on the God who has it all. I don't have to be overwhelmed by the enormity of it. However, I do need to admit when it's over my head. Even when my intentions are the best and most pure, if I don't step aside, I will fail. I will hurt those I am trying to help. If I don't enlist the resources God placed in my life, I am trying to play God. That doesn't work out well at all.

I also need to remember where I came from. In order to be strong in the Lord, I need to remember how far God has brought me in recovery and my spiritual walk. Not to place guilt and condemnation, but to bolster my faith in what more God can do. If I look around for examples of how to live, I will see that those who are loving the most, showing the most grace, are doing so because the Grace of God has been so perfectly shown them. And I need to admit I am "one of them".

There is a "thud" in the pit of my stomach when I truly understand the message: If I judge God based on my circumstances and how I think He should respond to them, then I am playing God. I am worshiping an idol made in my mind. I cannot judge God's character based on my circumstances. The things God knows and intends is a mystery, as well it should be, because He is God. I am not.

For me, it boils down to the fact I have a choice. I can be a fair-weather follower or I can be faithful. When I don't see the resources to accomplish the plan as I believe it to be, do I give up? Or do I keep believing in God's plan for the situation? Do I bow out or do

I ask God to show me the next step? I choose to believe God's love is never ending, never failing. This morning I choose faith when all else is unsure.

"Even from eternity I am He, And there is none who can deliver out of My hand; I act and who can reverse it?" (Isaiah 43:13)

"And looking at them Jesus said to them, 'With people this is impossible, but with God all things are possible.'" (Matthew 19:26)

Loving Silas

November 18, 2013

Wow! Talk about pumped up with faith.

I just got Silas home from visiting Decatur Christian School. When we rounded the corner to park the car, the entire school was lined up outside, cheering at the tops of their lungs. Once we were inside, each of the high school classes took turns praying over Silas. Those kids know how to pray. I can hear the faith, the passion, and the love they have for the Lord and for Silas in their words. Silas received *lots* of hugs.

Silas' sophomore class has organized fundraising. I'll say this: do not ever underestimate kids and what they can do when they pray and put their faith into action. Sign us: *Ready to face the giant.*

Silas Living With Cancer

We've always joked about it. Silas was a pre-school dropout. After only a month of three-year-old preschool, the teacher called me in for a discussion. She told me Silas wasn't ready for preschool yet. This had become all too apparent when the children went outside for recess. Silas had disappeared, only to be found back inside the classroom playing. If they were lining up for bathroom break, Silas might be in the lunchroom already.

Other such disappearing acts continued throughout Silas' life.

Silas once was shopping with his dad at Wal-Mart when suddenly he wasn't there. A Code-Adam alert was announced, with employees dispersed to find the missing toddler. Minutes later, Silas was found. He was safe. He was fine. He was in the deli. He explained, "I was hungry."

Extreme impulsivity. Single mindedness. This all made sense to Silas, whether it fit in with our plans or not.

Loving Silas

Silas spends hours on YouTube, following My Little Pony and Pokemon, and catching up on narratives about them. This was posted right after his initial surgery in November 2013. If you have any doubt about Silas' tenacious, hopeful attitude toward life, I hope his comments dispel it.

Silas Martin commented on a video on YouTube:
Shared publicly–Nov 19, 2013
"since wendsday I had surgery to remove a brain tumer. and I found out I have PNET cancer... i'm not really phased with this news when I was five I was diagnosed with cancer. can you draw 2 milotics chasing each other swimming in a circle?"

A "milotic" is a Pokemon character. Silas loves all things Pokemon. He loves talking on-line with other Pokemon fanatics. *Silas is not afraid of this brain tumor.*

Loving Silas

The tentative diagnosis is grade three or four PNET tumor. Brain tumors are not "staged," as other cancers are, but graded. Grade four is the most aggressive, the most deadly. PNET tumors are pretty rare, especially for a teenager. They usually are found in younger children. A PNET tumor in a patient with NF1 is virtually unheard of.

I sit down on the side of Silas' bed, and I read the odds to him. He looks me in the eyes and tells me he is going to be in the minority. He is not going to be a statistic. We recently heard a song on a Christian radio station about odds. The song is called, "Bigger Than the Odds," sung by Matt Vollmar and the Great Romance. That song has become our theme, something to cling to when the odds seem overwhelming:

Yesterday caught you off guard, Hitting harder than hitting a wall
The words that you don't want to hear, left you crippled and facing your fear
And you know now, The chance of survival is slim
And you know now, this feeling you're empty within

When it seems like all is lost
And you feel you can't go on
Just give it to a God
Who is bigger than the odds

Your aching heart falls to the floor, Your spirit can't take anymore
The numbness has washed over you, You're searching for more you could do
Cause you know now, The chance of survival is slim
And you know now, feeling like the whole world's caving in

When it seems like all is lost
And you feel you can't go on
Just give it to a God
Who is bigger than the odds
He gives strength to the weary and power to the weak

He's beyond understanding giving hope to the meek
To the ends of the earth, he is wherever we seek.

When it seems like all is lost
And you feel you can't go on
Just give it to a God
Who is bigger than the odds

"Bigger Than the Odds" used with permission from The Great Romance and Matt Vollmar

Loving Silas

November 26, 2013

Dear God, I don't understand. I don't change direction easily or quickly. However, I do know You are in control. Silas' oncologist called me this evening, after hours of discussion with his other doctors, to say they've hit the pause button. I have to say, "I don't get it, but okay, God." This feels like a roller coaster all over again.

They are not totally convinced what Silas' tumor is. It could be a PNET, or a Glioblastoma (GBM) or even something resulting from his earlier astrocytomas removed in 2006. Even though they are sure it is a grade four, treatment of the different types of tumors varies greatly. For instance, if it were GBM, he wouldn't have to have his spine exposed to radiation. If it were PNET, he'll have both spinal and brain radiation treatment.

God, I truly am thankful. They are checking out every single possibility, doing one last pathology test, and consulting more experts. I am thankful we have a long-standing relationship with this team; they have shown us over and over how committed they are to giving their everything to fight for my baby. I'm only being human, Lord. I'm selfish. I want a game plan. I'm so tired. I need to go cry in the shower and get it over with, so I can get back in the game.

You have carried us every step of the way, preparing us for this, and I know You will provide. I know You won't let us down now. Thank You for Your endless love, for the amazing prayer warriors who show up wherever we go—online, in person, and around every turn. Thank You for the hope we have, based on all You've done so far. Thank You my children know You, and their eternal future is secure in You. Forgive me when I complain or worry. I love You, for You are my "Daddy God." In Jesus' name, Amen.

Silas Living With Cancer

Silas was four years old. He was big for his age, although more wide than tall. I think he could have eaten us out of house and home, because he never felt "full." He always wanted more. He was always running to the kitchen for a snack.

His hunger was out of control. Silas literally had an insatiable appetite. We put locks on the refrigerator and the food cabinets, but his weight escalated.

In my gut, I knew something was wrong. I jokingly asked our pediatrician's nurse if they could look in his brain and see if something was wrong.

Loving Silas

November 30, 2013

I don't have to look far to find God speaking to me.

Silas and I will soon have to move close to St. Louis for Silas' daily radiation treatments. I'm feeling a little anxious as I pack up storage tubs and try to get my ducks in a row at home. I want my house to stay organized while we're away. As I opened our 2014 wall calendar, I started to throw away the cardboard support from inside . I stopped when I saw this timely message on that piece of cardboard trash:

"Just think, you're here not by chance, but by God's choosing. His hand formed you and made you the person you are. He compares you to no one else–you are one of a kind. You lack nothing that His grace can't give you. He has allowed you to be here at this time in history to fulfill His special purpose for this generation."

(Roy Lessin, DaySpring co-founder)

"To every thing there is a season, and a time to every purpose under the heaven." (Ecclesiastes 3:1)

Loving Silas

I've seen it on facebook many times. I've often thought about how true it actually is. I believe it. I'm on prayer chains, because I feel prayer should be our first line of defense, not our "backup plan":

"Sometimes we say, "All I can do is pray for you" ... but prayer isn't a concession. It is the single most powerful, most important thing you can do for another person." (Anon)

Loving Silas

December, 2013

We are settled in the basement of a friend's house in Wentzville, Missouri, so we're only forty-one miles away from Silas' daily radiation treatments. We've been working on making this feel like home. Silas has "wallpaper" of cards and posters, all hand made by his friends and classmates from Decatur Christian School. I have printed off many verses and spiritually inspiring quotes, and hung them in various groupings around our apartment. These are visual reminders of God's unfailing love for us.

Upstairs is a friendly dog named Toby, who gets lots of loving from Silas whenever we visit. It's chilly in the basement, but not cold. Silas chills easily, so Toby gets many visits.

We have a small bathroom with a shower. The bathroom doubles as our kitchen, for water, doing dishes, and such. We place space heaters strategically so Silas gets the maximum exposure to heat.

We know Silas is engaged in a battle for his life. I am keenly aware we are engaged in spiritual warfare as well. I thank God often for the many prayer warriors we have. I am lonely here. I try to keep everyone updated, communicating on facebook and posting pictures of Silas.

"God can do anything, you know—far more than you could ever imagine or guess or request in your wildest dreams! He does it not by pushing us around but by working within us, his Spirit deeply and gently within us.

Glory to God in the church!

Glory to God in the Messiah, in Jesus!

Glory down all the generations!

Glory through all millennia! Oh, yes!" (Ephesians 3:20-21 The Message)

Silas Living with Cancer

Silas has a brother named Shobi. Shobi is two years older, and smart as could be. With Silas' rapid growth, people often mistook the boys for fraternal twins.

The spring of 2004, both boys had allergy testing. Silas was sent for upper GI testing by the allergist. Two local tests showed Silas had multiple growths in the esophagus and possibly into the stomach. We were sent to a Springfield hospital for another upper GI which confirmed the previous tests. We were told these types of growths are common in patients who have NF.

Silas was scheduled for an endoscopy. We scheduled prayer. I e-mailed everyone I could think of. We made phone calls. We enlisted an army of prayer warriors.

At the hospital, the anesthesiologist identified herself as the wife of our pharmacist, and asked if she could pray over Silas before he went back for the procedure. Of course we consented.

In a short while, the doctor came out personally with photographs. His face showed bewilderment. He said, "I can't explain it. All those upper GI series. Here are the photographs. There are no growths there. There is nothing unusual."

This was a miracle, as far as we were concerned. We had no idea how much we would need to remember this miraculous healing in the years ahead.

Loving Silas

December 15, 2013

Silas update. We came home to Decatur for the weekend. The Holiday in the Halls Craft Fair was at DCS today. Both boys were with me and it was such a joy, despite the deep snow and frigid temperatures. Seeing so many people who pray for Silas is rewarding. I am so thankful for the financial support as well.

Silas' class has a special attitude: Stand By Silas.

They have made and sold gray ribbons and pins since early November. They established a special day each week when students may wear jeans instead of their uniforms in exchange for a donation to Silas' benefit account. Today they were selling ornaments and hand warmers and decorations. All of this is to support Silas' medical bills and our family's needs.

Later, I took Shobi shopping at the mall for warm clothing. I have missed that boy, even though we've only been gone a couple of weeks. I took Silas out to Latham for the Sophomore Christmas party. Silas was overjoyed to be doing normal things, and to be a part of his class again.

To top it off, I have extra "sometimes sons" sleeping on my couch tonight. I call them "sometimes sons" because I love them like sons. They are friends of my sons, who hang out at our home. They feel comfortable raiding the fridge. They know they are welcome here any time.

I am so blessed.

Loving Silas

December 22, 2013

How does this happen, Lord? In one week, how do I go from feeling so blessed, to feeling so stressed? How do I let my fear overcome my faith? How do I get to the point where I don't want to feel? When did I quit trusting You this week?

How many times this week have I gone through the motions, getting Silas back and forth to his radiation treatments, only to come home and lie motionless on my bed, unwilling to do anything but the bare minimum? Unwilling to form a thought, let alone call someone and talk. Not that I know what I would have said.

I have been sober almost three years, God. Why would I try to numb myself now, instead of walking through the sea of roiling emotions inside of me?

I am so ashamed of myself.

"Save me, O God, for the waters have come up to my neck. I sink in the miry depths, where there is no foothold. I have come into the deep waters; the floods engulf me. I am worn out calling for help; my throat is parched. My eyes fail, looking for my God." (Psalm 69:1-3)

Silas Living With Cancer

Because Silas had problems with preschool, and because he had experienced delays, we were blessed to enroll him in Lollipops pre-kindergarten. This program was specially designed for children at risk of not being ready for kindergarten when it was age appropriate. His class was at our local public school, and Silas rode the bus.

Silas had strong feelings of right and wrong. It might take him a while to learn a concept, but once he did, it was ingrained.

One day when the bus driver dropped off Silas in front of our house, he handed me a note. The note informed me that Silas was in danger of losing his bus-riding privileges. It went on to explain what happened.

One hard and fast rule is school buses in Illinois stop at every railroad crossing. Another hard and fast rule is when the bus stops at a crossing, all children must sit down immediately. Apparently, the boy in the seat ahead of Silas remained standing when the bus came to a stop at the train tracks. Silas took it upon himself to "enforce" the rule. Because Silas was bigger than the other children, he had no problem taking his classmate by the shoulders and *making* him sit in his seat, along with several words of harsh reprimand.

We chuckled a bit at the driver's recollection of what happened, and it became a favorite "Silas story" in our family. We had to wonder, though, at what prompted such outbursts, as this was not an isolated incident.

Loving Silas

December 24, 2013

We stayed after Silas' radiation treatment to meet with the nurse, who gave Silas more laxatives. We stopped at a mall west of St. Louis on our way back to our basement abode. It is a huge mall.

While strolling past the stores into the food court, Silas suddenly started running for the restrooms. I pointed him in the right direction, but he was running. By himself. Using his white cane.

I wish I could have snapped a picture of the crowds he parted. The looks on people's faces were priceless as this "blind" person ran at them.

Anyway, the outcome was good. Thank you everyone. Keep praying for regularity in that department. This is only one of the nasty side effects of Silas' chemotherapy.

Have a wonderful Christmas Eve.

Loving Silas

December 25, 2013

We had the most amazing Christmas Dinner and visit. Silas' dad and Shobi met Silas and me in Collinsville, Illinois. The restaurant treated us to dinner. We had awesome service, we opened gifts, and oh, how we laughed! I returned to Wentzville with both boys. Shobi is going to stay with us for a few days here.

Silas takes the time to read every single card made and sent to him, as long as it is printed and not in cursive writing. We received a package of cards sent by Ms. Birch's 4th grade at French Academy back home, sent via a Basket of Hope, who also sent lots of uplifting gifts for Silas. Thank you for all the Christmas Cards sent. Silas wants me to hang them up here to see always. Both boys went with me to an open AA meeting as well. This truly has been a Merry Christmas.

"So Joseph also went up from the town of Nazareth in Galilee to Judea, to Bethlehem the town of David, because he belonged to the house and line of David. He went there to register with Mary, who was pledged to be married to him and was expecting a child. While they were there, the time came for the baby to be born, and she gave birth to her firstborn, a son. She wrapped him in cloths and placed him in a manger, because there was no guest room available for them.

And there were shepherds living out in the fields nearby, keeping watch over their flocks at night. An angel of the Lord appeared to them, and the glory of the Lord shone around them, and they were terrified. But the angel said to them, "Do not be afraid. I bring you good news that will cause great joy for all the people. Today in the town of David a Savior has been born to you; he is the Messiah, the Lord. This will be a sign to you: You will find a baby wrapped in cloths and lying in a manger."

Suddenly a great company of the heavenly host appeared with the angel, praising God and saying, 'Glory to God in the highest heaven, and on earth peace to those on whom his favor rests.'" (Luke 2:4-14)

Silas Living with Cancer

When Silas started losing teeth about the time he turned five, we didn't give it much thought. After all, Shobi was losing teeth. They were losing teeth together. If I remember correctly, Silas had lost nearly eight teeth by the end of Kindergarten. Also at the end of Kindergarten, Silas' reading level had started falling. An appointment was set for me to meet with his Kindergarten teacher to plan how best to help Silas.

Before that appointment, Silas met with an ophthalmologist. As parents of a child with NF1, we had taken Silas for these exams every eighteen months or so since he was two years old. She noticed something different with his optic nerves than she had seen in past exams. We knew to watch for these changes. These changes could possibly indicate brain tumors. She referred Silas for an MRI at St. Louis Children's Hospital, where there also is an NF Clinic.

I went to the conference with Silas' Kindergarten teacher. I knew then Silas' vision had become impaired, and had contributed to his declining grades. I remember crying and praying with her.

Loving Silas

December 28, 2013

Silas' hair started falling out tonight, a patch in the back, apparently from radiation therapy. I want to cry, because this is only the start. I want to laugh, too, because this is exactly what Silas wanted from the very first treatment for brain tumors in 2004. He heard this is a possible side effect of chemotherapy. He wanted to be bald. Back then, he endured roughly three years of chemo, and he never lost his hair. Three weeks of radiation treatments, and it looks like he'll get his wish.

Loving Silas

I'm thinking back. Was it only 3 months ago? Shobi was having his senior pictures taken. I convinced both boys to go, and we took both of our dogs.

Bobby is our old man, a German Shepherd and Doberman mix. We've had him since 2004. Posh is our new girl, a Great Dane, about six years old. We were blessed to adopt her from a wonderful, rapidly expanding family. While in our family, she's had a few surgeries, including amputation of a rear leg due to bone cancer. Posh and Silas have an incredible bond. She loves us all, but she loves Silas most of all. Since osteosarcoma is so aggressive, and we don't know how long Posh will be around, we decided to have family pictures done the same day as Shobi's senior pix.

Now, I have to wonder if God wasn't directing us that day for an entirely different reason. I have started to wonder how long Silas will be with us. I don't dare say those words out loud.

Silas Living With Cancer

Many of the quirky things we thought made Silas unique were, in fact, symptoms of brain tumors. Specifically, he had Optic Pathway Gliomas. These tumors were at the chiasm, the crossing of the optic nerves at the base of the brain. They also were pressing on the Pituitary Gland and the Hypothalamus.

Silas was visually impaired. He had precocious puberty. The impulsivity, circadian rhythm disturbance, obesity and more were all caused by the brain tumors. In an instance, it all made sense. This curse, this plague, this cause had a name. Silas had turned six years old. Silas had brain tumors.

This is an excerpt from a mass e-mail sent August 26, 2004:

"We thank you for your prayers for Silas. We also ask that you continue to pray for him. He is expected to go through 14 months of chemotherapy. He'll go every week for the first 12 weeks, then several "rounds" of 4 weeks "on" and 3 weeks "off". The side effects can vary, but include painful mouth sores, constipation, depleted immune system, and more. The doctors' goal is to stop the growth of the tumors, and essentially turn them into scar tissue.

Another issue is to address the precocious puberty the tumors have caused due to the location on the hypothalamus. Tests run in St. Louis show his body is that of a nine-year-old. He must receive a monthly painful injection to stop the hormonal growth, and let his body and brain catch up.

You know what, though? All this is answered prayer. We have long wondered about his size, we have long wondered about his speech delays, we have long wondered why he wakes fully in the middle of the night, raring to go. Knowing about this brain tumor is like a hand wrapped gift straight from heaven.

And Silas? He is the most awesome patient in the world. We do well to take our lead from this. Silas totally trusts that God is in control. God may allow this, but did not order it for him. He also remains the most incredibly loving child."

For Silas, we had embarked on a grand adventure. I was terrified.

I vowed to be there for him no matter what. I wanted to present a strong front for him, but most importantly, I wanted him to know my strength comes from a saving relationship with Jesus Christ. After a few conversations, he asked to be baptized before he went to St. Louis for his first surgery. Our pastor kindly consented, even though we all wondered at his ability to understand.

Loving Silas

December 30, 2013

Dear Carey,

I know you're my supervisor, but I've grown to confide in you as well. It's funny, I had all these grand expectations that I would work by remote laptop at least four hours each day down here, because Silas' treatments were all scheduled early to mid-morning. I assumed of course I would be Super Mom / Super Woman, and not feel any of the stress of being sole caretaker, or that of being totally isolated from adult human life form most every day. I also didn't know Silas' condition and care for him would consume me.

Early on, when this started in November, I remember you saying you wouldn't want to hear from or about work, if you were in my shoes. At that point, I really don't think it had hit me this time is so very different from all the other cancers and conditions Silas has gone through before. It took being down here and living through this, to actually walk through it, in order for me to understand and digest the situation. You are so wise. I didn't know.

Even the constant driving can take its toll, can't it? Even the packing and unpacking to travel with a kid on lots of meds is stressful.

What I'm trying to say is, thank you. Thank you to everyone who knows I am still here, even though I haven't been able to work much at all. Thank you to everyone who has donated vacation days so I am still able to pay the mortgage and the power bill back home. Thank you to you, for your suggestion from the beginning of this mess, when you told me to take a deep breath, and not worry about work. You said it would all work out, and there was no need for me to panic.

Like I said, you were right.

Loving Silas

December 31, 2013

For the first time on this journey starting November 3rd, 2013, Silas is grumpy. It's only Tuesday, and he is tired, and he's worried about feeling grumpy on Thursday when he goes back after a day off. He'll have radiation AND chemotherapy AND both doctor exams. I told him it's okay to be grumpy, and that I won't push him to figure out what's wrong, if he'll be honest with me. Sometimes we feel grumpy, and if that's the case, tell me. I think we have a deal. He also started having pain right behind his right ear today.

I'm hoping he'll perk up after a shower and washing his patches of hair. We're packing up to go to the Leaps of Love New Year's Eve retreat. It is a superhero themed pajama party. I'm ready for some laughter with some kids who are definitely superheroes.

Silas Living with Cancer

Some things don't make sense. I shake my head in wonder, because I can't figure them out.

We've discovered along with Silas' visual loss, he is color blind. That just doesn't make any sense. You see, Silas' favorite board game is CandyLand.

Loving Silas

January 20, 2014

Fifteen years ago, I would not have been saying this, but today I am thankful for my child who wakes me in the middle of the night. How long would his brain tumor have gone undiagnosed, if Silas had not awakened me at 2:22 a.m. November 3rd last year?

Last night at 1:57 am, he woke me to tell me how hungry he was. He was *energized* and wanted a milkshake made with Boost and a Steak & Shake chocolate malt. Other nights, I am so thankful prayers are answered, and he wakes me to tell me he pooped.

I know it sounds silly, but I am thankful today. I am thankful you ask what to pray for, and you sincerely want to pray specifically for Silas. You are sincere and genuine, and you're not offended by any of Silas' needs.

This morning, walking into the treatment room, he cracked his head on an overhead cabinet. He has no concussion that we know of. We iced it, and he's had no real head pain. However, Silas' back is aching quite a bit. Apparently, this is a side effect of radiology treatments. He's going to take a break now, playing his new 3DS game he bought at Best Buy with a Christmas gift card. Have a blessed day.

"In every thing give thanks: for this is the will of God in Christ Jesus concerning you." (1 Thessalonians 5:18)

Loving Silas

January 23, 2014

Silas rang the bell today to commemorate his last day of radiation treatment! Traci and Alicia from Leaps Of Love were here to help us celebrate, despite the subzero temperatures. Silas and I will head back to Decatur on Friday. We have two days of appointments in St. Louis next week, then clinic, blood work, and MRI scans a week later. Silas' first week of in-patient chemotherapy starts in four weeks, then every third week for almost a year. Silas needs prayers against all the side effects that have left him "zapped". He's eating pretty well, but needs to put some pounds back on.

When I look at my son, I'm starting to understand how devastating the treatment has been. Silas has lost more than weight. He has lost the ability to stay awake all day. He can no longer run. The distance he can even walk has diminished drastically. Silas now has foot drop as a result of one of the chemo drugs. He tries valiantly to walk as much as I ask, because he realizes he must move muscles to retain them.

At home, Silas can no longer walk up the stairs to his bedroom. We have had to make room for Silas and me to sleep on the main floor. To do this, I've sorted out many of my clothes to give to charity. I have way too many anyway. Silas' bed is moved to the dining room. I will sleep in the hanging hammock chair next to him, or on the couch in the living room. I am not comfortable being too far away from him.

I know it may not seem like a loss, but I hate that my "Mr. Independent" has lost so much of his independence. He needs me for so much, like taking a shower and helping with meals. He used to relish being "hands off." Not so much anymore. He wants help and never complains. Silas never cries. He never shows if it bothers him. I learn from that. I will talk with someone else I trust. I won't go there with Silas, no matter how furious I am at his losses.

Then, as I'm resting near him tonight, before falling to sleep, Silas whispers to me, "Just trust God. Just trust God."

Silas Living With Cancer

I listened to and sang with praise tapes when the boys were little. Yes, cassette tapes. Tapes of Bible verses put to music. It helped me to memorize them. I might not have known chapter and verse, but I could sing them word for word.

One of these is Isaiah 40:31, with an added prayer:

"...they that wait upon the Lord shall renew their strength; they shall mount up with wings as eagles; they shall run, and not be weary; they shall walk, and not faint. Teach me Lord, Teach me Lord, to wait."

That verse is also on a refrigerator magnet. Silas appropriately called it, "the magnet." From the time Silas was about three years old, he would run to the fridge, point to it, and say, "Sing the magnet! Sing the magnet!" to anyone, and everyone.

We have hilarious memories of him doing that to random guests who had no idea what he was talking about. An explanation always ensued, along with "singing of the magnet."

Without even knowing that he was doing so, Silas was spreading the Good News.

Loving Silas

February 21, 2014

Silas is in the middle of five days of in-patient chemotherapy. I received a phone call from one of the employees here at SLCH, coordinating the purchase of a wheelchair and a walker. I had just heard from Physical Therapy they want Silas to have both accommodations until he becomes more mobile again.

I was feeling a little overwhelmed at this news, so I'd started reading Psalm 91 when the phone rang. The conversation started like this: "Hi, this is So&So with St. Louis Children's Hospital. I coordinate providers for equipment. I want you to know I am praying for your son, and I know this must be a really challenging time for you as well." She went on about the business part, and ended the conversation with prayers for blessings on Silas.

Very cool. How did she even know how her prayers would be received? God knows my needs before I do.

"He will cover you with his feathers, and under his wings you will find refuge; his faithfulness will be your shield and rampart." (Psalm 91:4)

Loving Silas

February 24, 2014

We finally left SLCH at 4:30 p.m. today. Silas is so glad to be home with his Posh. He weathered his first in-patient chemo well. God has blessed him with such a positive attitude and resilience against side effects of chemo so far. He is very motivated to get his legs strong again. We have a schedule of physical therapy exercises and outings, including going to Decatur Memorial Hospital for blood draws twice a week. He truly wants to be "Mr. Independent" again. Thank you all for the continued prayers and love.

Silas Living with Cancer

I don't know when it happened, but Jeremiah 29:11 became Silas' life verse. He would tell you that. He wanted a wall plaque of it near him where he slept. He believed God had a future for him.

From the e-mail I sent out December 1, 2005: "Silas finished up chemotherapy four weeks ago, and had an MRI today at St. Louis Children's Hospital to see what the next "step" is. Endocrinology doctor determined that the hormone shots (Lupron) Silas receives every three weeks is keeping the precocious puberty at bay. No new symptoms other than he is the only second grader at his school that absolutely must use deodorant. He will continue to receive Lupron shots until he is of an age that puberty normally would have occurred, probably between twelve and fourteen years old.

Preliminary results of the MRI: the tumor size has remained constant; however there are new "areas" highlighted by the contrast dye. We were told it is too early to worry, so we are not doing so. Besides, my best friend, Eileen told me worry is concern without prayer.

Silas' IEP (Individual Education Plan) through the public school district is providing him with wonderful assistance. Four times per week, Silas leaves his Christian school early, and we take him to one of the public schools in Decatur which has an incredible low-vision lab, where he meets up with his vision teacher. Since early in September until now, Silas has mastered reading and "writing" (on the Brailler) all of the letters of the alphabet, all the numbers, and many symbols. He is starting on many of the 196 "contractions" that each have a symbol in Braille. He delights in "reading" the Braille on public restroom doors.

He is learning to use a "spy glass" or telescope, called a monocular, so he will be able to see the blackboard finally, or on stage for a play or assembly, or a hot-air balloon in the distance when we are traveling in the car. Are these actually little things in life? Plus, the doctor emphasized to us something we never thought of. He explained the ultimate importance of protecting Silas' one "good" eye, the eye that sees much better than the other. If something happened to it, he would be truly blind. As a result of the discussion, she ordered protective glasses. One is a wrap-around really cool pair of "rec specs" that look like motorcycle rider "shades " The other is a "dress" pair, to be used when he is not in physical activities.

Silas is excelling in school, even on the honor roll first quarter, with all As and Bs. We are very proud of him. He has a great attitude. He loves learning about Jesus at school. His teacher is wonderful.

Thank you for your continued prayers. We feel them. Praise God for His blessings, especially His prayer warriors."

"For I know the plans I have for you," declares the Lord, "plans to prosper you and not to harm you, plans to give you hope and a future." (Jeremiah 29:11)

Loving Silas

March 2, 2014

Silas had a rough night sleeping. He woke up around 5 a.m. then went back to sleep around 9 a.m. He wanted the couch, so I snoozed on his bed. Later, when we both were finally up moving around, I heard a loud Boom! in the bathroom. Silas had gone down, folded into a pretzel shape on the half-bath floor. All he was trying to do was pick up a piece of trash. He has lost so much strength and agility, he couldn't hold himself up to do so. My heart breaks.

Thank You, God, for a gait belt. I was able to get him up again. It looks like we need to persist with those exercises.

Loving Silas

"...Rejoice always; pray without ceasing; in everything give thanks; for this is God's will for you in Christ Jesus...." (1 Thessalonians 5:16-18)

I read it. I know what it says. But come on, God: *pray without ceasing*? How is that even possible? The more I think about it, the more I know God was serious when He put that in the Word. I know I better figure this one out.

If I don't think I can pray all the time, when can I pray?

Sure, I devote time to God first thing in the morning. Wait. My devotions aren't actually first thing. They always come *after* I've let the dogs out, after I've tended to Silas' needs. I guess I could use that time with the dogs to start praying. After all, it only takes a few seconds to shoot a prayer up. So I tell myself, "Every time you pick up those leashes, talk to God." It may take a while to make it a habit, but I can start today.

The next thing I do each day is get dressed. When I pull on my clothes, I can thank God for clothing me in the robes of righteousness. There's a thanksgiving prayer right there. And as I help Silas get dressed, we can talk about how God covers us. Again, it may take a while to form the habit, but I can start today.

What are some of the other things I do daily, or several times throughout the day? Keys. I have keys to my car, keys to my house, keys to cabinets and drawers at work. I can pray aloud with Silas as I turn the key in the car or the back door of our house. What a great prompt to pray.

If I would simply start praying whenever I pick up the dogs' leashes, whenever I put on or take off an article of clothing, and whenever I see or use a key, I would be praying so much more than before. And I would be so much closer to following God's command.

Suddenly, I realize I can read those verses and make excuses. Or I can read those verses, and ask God to remind me, whatever memory techniques I conjure up.

Yes, there's another one. God, whenever I start making excuses, please remind me to pray.

Silas Living with Cancer

Early 2006

The MRI showed more tumors. These were astrocytomas. Typical for NF1 patients, and non-malignant. The problem with any brain tumor is something must be done. Whether it is malignant or benign is not the question. If allowed to grow uncontrolled inside the skull, sooner or later it will kill.

Before surgery to resect the tumors, Silas looked at his neurosurgeon long and hard. Quietly he asked, "While I'm asleep for surgery, would you please shave my head so I'm bald like you?" His sly smile was barely discernible. Only Silas...

Silas was home, eating hot dogs within four days of surgery. Unheard of short recovery times became Silas' trademark.

Loving Silas

March 6, 2014

I just finished reading a book about being the primary caregiver for a "cancer kid." I suddenly feel normal.

I sleep on the couch in yesterday's clothes. I wake up to the yowls of canine and feline stomachs when I'm home. When at the hospital, the sounds of IV pumps are like lullabies. I realize I use the pronoun "we" instead of "I" when talking about trips to the hospital now. I realize how utterly helpless I am without God.

I am so totally blessed by my recovery and church families. They often step in to do whatever is needed. Once again, like Silas' song, I am going to "...Give it to our God, Who is bigger than the odds."

Loving Silas

Mid March, 2014

Silas continues with in-patient chemotherapy. While in the hospital, he receives physical therapy. The therapists say Silas has made amazing progress in the last two weeks. He has regained symmetrical strength, in his arms and legs, but he still needs to work on ankle exercises and balance. When we get home, if anyone wants to visit to exercise with Silas, please do. We asked social services to look into home health care, but it doesn't look like it will pan out. If we could get it approved, I could go back to work three weeks each month.

Much bigger news came today. The Physicians Assistant at SLCH warned us the last shot of his current round of chemo would cost $900 out of pocket. She came back only one hour later to tell us it will be $30 out of pocket. Can you believe that? God is amazing.

I don't know why I'm amazed when God does something so simple as reduce a medical bill by $870. God has done so many other more amazing things in our lives. He has helped me attain sobriety again. He has allowed Silas to overcome so many obstacles in his life. He has given Silas fast and furious healing from craniotomies. If I want to be amazed, I need only look back to the Spring of 2004, when God healed Silas of multiple growths in his esophagus. Today is chump change for my God!

This month brought a lung infection, shingles, blood transfusions, another air lift to St. Louis and seven different hospitalizations for Silas. All the while, he has had such a good outlook. He insists on having his My Little Pony blanket with him. His classmates sent it to him a while back. He is a Brony, through and through.

Many times I wake up at the hospital with a hymn or a praise song in my thoughts. Recently, I was so caught up in worry and anxiety, I couldn't "hear" a single one. I called a dear friend in the middle of the night, and asked her to sing to me. Sarah has the sweetest, clearest voice. Later, she posted these words on my facebook timeline as well:

"Why should I feel discouraged?
Why should the shadows come?
Why should my heart feel lonely

And long for heaven and home?
For Jesus is my portion.
A constant friend is He.
His eye is on the sparrow
And I know He watches me.
His eye is on the sparrow
And I know He watches me.
I sing because I'm happy.
I sing because I'm free.
For His eye is on the sparrow
And I know He watches me." *(His Eye is On the Sparrow: lyricist Civilla D. Martin and composer Charles H. Gabriel)*

I know I've prayed this before, but God, please, let my faith be greater than my fear.

Silas Living With Cancer

June 20, 2007

I wrote to friends: "Silas is enjoying a pretty normal life now. He had an MRI April 26th showing his three brain tumors were dormant for about six months, so his last dose of chemotherapy was 5/2/07. He lost ten pounds immediately, and his energy level went up as well. His sleep pattern is more normal, and he *loves* to tell people he has "graduated" from chemo."

Silas started getting mailings and invitations about camps. Some were organized by medical staff specializing in cancer treatment. Some were specific for students who are visually impaired or blind. Some were church camps. Silas wanted to go to all of them.

The first time I dropped Silas off at Illinois School for the Visually Impaired, I acted as if I'd never see him again. Silas, on the other hand, was oblivious to the fact I was still there. He had found a world where all the kids around him were like him. He was no longer different. He was busy comparing notes, making friends. He was accepted.

Loving Silas

April, 2014

I know this couch is only six feet away from Silas. It feels like miles. I sleep best right beside my son. I know his pain and when he needs meds. I know his grimaces, his gasping. I am not about to take the time for a shower. I don't even carry makeup anymore. All I want is for my son to have some relief. I've posted the need, so please pray. Now, I am going back to my spot beside Silas. If I'm not there, he asks me to come back and hold him.

I've been thinking about the unrelenting stress of the last month, and wondering if I did everything I could to help Silas through it all. When I start to wonder, I tend to doubt myself, and lean toward lies I believed in my past. Lies we tell ourselves or others tell us, are at the root of shame. We all have shame, it is universal and one of the most primitive human emotions we experience. Shame is a lie from Hell. It says we are mistakes, and attacks the character and identity with lies we somehow believe to be truth.

I am a child of God, a bigger and better identity of who I am. I make mistakes. God picks me up and makes me stronger in Him. I am thankful for a peace from God.

"Do not be anxious about anything, but in everything, by prayer and petition, with thanksgiving present your requests to God. And the *peace of God*, which transcends all understanding, will guard your hearts and minds in Christ Jesus." (Philippians 4:6-7)

Silas has been weaned off IV pain meds, and we are learning to use extended release oral pain meds, with break-thru oral meds as well. Shingles are gone, but the pain and itching persist. Gabapentin will help as well, and will be prophylactic when he starts on the chemo which causes neuropathy. We will be able to manage that at home, after Friday when this round of chemotherapy is over. We move to 9th floor in the morning to start chemo. He is so motivated to stay hydrated because they reduced the IV fluids as well. I am so proud of him. So filled with gratitude for his faith. He prays for so many other people as soon as he hears the need. Thank you all for your patience with all these updates. Thank you for your love and prayers for this little (not so little) warrior.

Through many donations and endless hours of devotion from Silas' classmates, we have enough in Silas' Benefit Account to cover most of the cost of remodeling. Silas and I will stay at a local hotel while contractors construct a bedroom and full bath where we once had a family room and half bath. I have conceded Silas will never get strong enough to handle stairs at home again. I have conceded sponge baths aren't enough for a fifteen-year-old young man.

I have given up hope our lives will ever return to what they were before this brain tumor.

Loving Silas

April 13, 2014

It was wonderful to be in church today with Silas. It was a great sermon.

I think Silas is busy confusing non-believers, and those who say, "How does he keep such a great attitude?" and "Why isn't he having more side effects?" or "Why would he give a gift card to someone else, instead of using it himself?"

I'll answer all of those questions. He's a believer. He believes in Jesus. He has a joy that can't be squelched by adversity. He believes in a God who is bigger than the odds.

Loving Silas

Silas has been so tired the last couple of days. He didn't want to wake up to go to breakfast. Yes, I made him walk all the way there and back. He didn't want to take a bath. Yes, I made him do it and get up out of the tub on his own. He didn't want to get up and go to DMH for regular Monday blood work. Yes, I made him.

He did, however, want to go with all his gift cards and money he's saved up, to buy an iPod 5th generation. Yes, I took him, although I did not allow him to use a wheelchair. He needs to walk to strengthen his legs. I hate being the heavy all the time, but I saw how happy he was with his purchase. Instead of a drive-thru for lunch, he even got out of the car to build his own sandwich at a sub shop afterwards.

Silas is getting around so well with his walker. He stands so straight and tall, as long as I tell him what is ahead, like bumps and rugs. Remember, he isn't able to use his white cane for low vision, while using the walker to help him get around. I have to be his eyes. I have to keep hold of his gait belt behind, in case he goes down suddenly. We've learned to work together well. He is such a trooper.

It is increasingly difficult do this. It is harder each day to be me, loving Silas, and separate myself from Silas living with cancer. Somewhere along the journey, our paths have become one, and I am now Loving Silas Living With Cancer.

Silas Living With Cancer

Silas had a propensity for questions. He had a raging curiosity about how and why things work the way they do. He also liked to try to figure out the answers to those questions himself. He called these actions experiments.

It was a regular occurrence to find something unusual in the freezer. I don't mean only an unusual food. Silas did that. He wanted to know what frozen grapes, bananas, and candy bars were like. He also wanted to know if one could freeze an egg. He made the common mistake of freezing a can of soda pop, which I cleaned for months. It was not unusual to find non-food items in our freezer as well, like dryer lint he soaked before freezing.

Some of his experiments took him outside. He had to see if table salt actually dried up slugs. He had me make homemade weed killer, then watched to see how long it took to be effective.

One day, I pulled into our drive and got out, only to find a strange slimy mess on the sidewalk, with white granules sprinkled all around it. I knew who to ask. Silas confessed the television weatherman had said it was "so hot outside you can fry an egg on the pavement." He had to try. He even salted them so they'd taste good.

Loving Silas

I am trying to have a good attitude about the "accommodations" Silas must have. I asked him a couple of days ago if he resents having to use a walker. He said, "No, I'm just thankful it helps me get around." So, as I look to today and Silas receiving his AFO leg braces, I am trying to not be sad Silas isn't able to run with only his white cane, like he could a year ago. I am trying not to think of the things I thought he would have accomplished in the last few months, had he not had this brain tumor. I am asking God to help me see the leg braces and be thankful they will strengthen his ankles. I am asking God to give me a grateful heart, and to rejoice in all the miracles in Silas' life thus far. I am reminded Silas has a pure, grateful heart. I want to be more like Silas.

"And he said unto me, My grace is sufficient for thee: for my strength is made perfect in weakness. Most gladly therefore will I rather glory in my infirmities, that the power of Christ may rest upon me." (2 Corinthians 12:9)

Loving Silas

Jeremiah 45:5 was the first subject Silas and I discussed this morning. "But you, are you seeking great things for yourself? Jesus said, 'Ask, and it will be given to you; seek, and you will find; knock, and it will be opened to you.'" (Matthew 7:7)

What are you asking for and why? Ask yourself these questions. Are you following God to get what you want, or are you following God to do what *He* wants? These two things may be incredibly different from each other.

God knows what you need before you ask. God's ultimate plan for you is complete joy and peace, but it may come to you in an unexpected way.

Father in heaven, thank You for giving me strength to overcome every obstacle in life. I choose to rejoice no matter what may come against me. I know You are working all things together for my good in Jesus' name. Amen.

Loving Silas

SLCH Hem Onc Clinic called. All of Silas' blood counts are fantastic.

This takes the cake, though. While walking down the hall at DMH to the lab today, Silas asked, "Mom, what are you going to do with the handicap placard for the car when I don't need it anymore?" Isn't that awesome? Not *if* he doesn't need it anymore, but *when* he doesn't need it anymore. I want some more of his attitude.

"Have I not commanded you? Be strong and courageous! Do not tremble or be dismayed, for the LORD your God is with you wherever you go." (Joshua 1:9)

Silas Living With Cancer

From an e-mail sent out October 4, 2007: "Can you say, '*Remission*?!'

Silas had his MRI yesterday. Today he saw his team of doctors. We got the phone call tonight with good news. The astrocytomas in his right temporal lobe and the left half of the basal ganglia are "better." That means they are not smaller, but do not show up as bright on the MRI. This indicates no activity. The right half of the Basal Ganglia and his Optic Pathway Gliomas are unchanged from the last two MRI scans, which means they are still as bright, but are not any brighter or bigger. All during a period of *no chemotherapy*.

This kind of progress is phenomenal. His St. Louis team is pleased and commented on how well he looks and acts. He did have a slight seizure recently, so he will continue with anti-seizure medicine indefinitely. Academically, he is doing extremely well, and has been moved back into the main classroom for a longer portion of his school day.

This is a good day."

Loving Silas

Breathe in God; Breathe out anxiety.
Breathe in God; Breathe out fear.
Breathe in God; Breathe out stress.
Breathe in God...
Breathe in God...

Loving Silas

The days in the month of May, 2014 all run together. Silas is doing so well with chemotherapy. I'm back to work at Ameren Illinois most days except when taking Silas to St. Louis. Because insurance isn't going to cover a paid caregiver, I hired one of my "sometimes sons," Keith to be Silas' companion. Keith is a win-win. Not only does Silas love his friend, Keith is as good as any certified caregiver. He is compassionate and disciplined enough to give Silas his meds on time. He makes certain Silas eats and does his exercises, and he still has time to play videogames with Silas.

I am so grateful for work. It distracts me. It provides a paycheck. I need work. I'm still uneasy being away from Silas. I feel a part of me is missing when I'm not with him.

I wonder if God longs for me to be with Him when I wander. I find the answer in His Word: "Therefore the LORD longs to be gracious to you, And therefore He waits on high to have compassion on you. For the LORD is a God of justice; How blessed are all those who long for Him." (Isaiah 30:18)

Loving Silas

June 15, 2014

What a weekend. Children's Wishing Well Foundation of St. Louis provided Silas a weekend away at Arch Anime' Convention in Collinsville, Illinois. There were lots of Pokemon activities. There were lots of My Little Pony activities. There were discussion panels, video games, and more. Many people wore costumes of their favorite characters. Silas was in heaven.

Silas chose Blake and Keith to accompany us. We all were overwhelmed at the swag bags in the hotel when we arrived. We were treated like celebrities, with photo opportunities with the *real* famous people.

Silas loves Chinese and Japanese food, and he received a gift card from a local restaurant (Asia House) where we dined all weekend. What an honor and privilege to share time with these fine young men.

This weekend was priceless. Silas says it was better than Make A Wish 10 years ago!

The Children's Wishing Well Foundation of St. Louis, is an all volunteer locally run charity that grants wishes to chronically and terminally ill children. 12901 N 40 Dr, St. Louis, MO 63141 (314) 523-6980

Silas Living with Cancer

In March, 2008, a student teacher working on a project asked for detailed information about Silas in preparation for one-on-one research. Here are parts of my response:

We are more than happy to help out with your project. Here are our responses to your questions:

What does your child enjoy doing at home?

Silas loves to play PS2 games such as Ben Ten Protector of Earth and Lego Star Wars 2. Even though he has to get close to play/see, he actually is pretty good at them. He also enjoys playing on our Personal Computer. Both of these are privileges he earns by being responsible at home and school. One of his most favorite things to do is to "play" Scrabble. He will sit on the floor for a long time, creating words on the Scrabble board. He likes to go through magazines for recipes to prepare at home as well. He enjoys exploring the backyard. One thing he enjoys doing at home that is a frustration to his parents is doing 'experiments' without prior parental permission. The results are sometimes messy–sometimes hilarious–sometimes quite creative.

What are your child's likes and dislikes?

Silas likes to be independent. He likes to 'check off' his duties on charts at home. He especially likes a sense of accomplishment. He doesn't like it when he is kept from doing something because someone underestimates his abilities. He doesn't like it when someone tells him something on one day, and the next day it doesn't happen or come true. He doesn't like misunderstandings, and considers them as lies. He likes people, especially those younger than himself. He doesn't like loud noises, especially yelling.

How well does your child use their vision?

I think Silas uses his vision very well. Although his reading and education will always need adaptation, I think Silas is able to use his vision in his left (good) eye to an extent that he will continue to achieve honor roll status in regular, public school, and be gainfully employed as an adult. He enjoys "spying" things far off you might not expect him to be able to see. I don't know if it is his vision or his sense of location / direction, but Silas has always had an ability to remember how to navigate to places he might only have been driven to one time. And, even though he uses his vision as a primary sense, he is strong at thinking abstractly, doing math in his head.

How efficient is your child at home?

Efficient is a subjective term. Silas is efficient in remembering what his responsibilities are and when they are to be done. Silas is efficient in following specific directions. On the other hand, Silas' ability to make a bed would probably be labeled as less than efficient by my own childhood's standards. Silas' ability to answer the telephone in a responsible manner is highly efficient, although his message-taking is lacking, due to inexperience. Silas is highly motivated by personal benefit. Silas is very efficient navigating in our home and in familiar places.

Does the child have siblings? If so, do they get along?

Silas has a brother named Shobi (Pr: Show-Bee) who is eleven (11). He and Silas are almost exactly two (2) years apart. Their sibling rivalry has been delayed somewhat, in my own personal opinion, due to Silas' approximately three years of medical complications due to brain tumors, chemotherapy, surgeries, hospitalizations, and such. They seem fairly normal: we used to joke they each had a favorite toy, which was whatever the other boy was playing with! Only after Silas was in remission did their sibling rivalry get started, and I think they've made up for lost time now. They can fight like cats & dogs. However, if as parents, we are consistent with clear expectations and consequences, both boys treat each other with civility and usually get along. They, naturally, fight over "stuff"–but if either one is in danger or sick, the other boy is right there, offering comfort and love.

Silas also has a sister, Kristin, "Sissy", who is twenty-one (21) years old. She was twelve (12) when Silas was born, and helped a great deal with him because he was such a fussy baby. She loves to spoil her baby brother. HOWEVER, she also expects a great deal from Silas, and doesn't cut him any special 'breaks' because of his visual impairment. As a result, he respects her authority and responds to her consistent manner. She doesn't live with us now, but did until about 4 years ago.

What are your child's strengths and weaknesses?

Silas is very compassionate, caring and respectful. He has a positive outlook on life, is laid back, and pretty much 'goes with the flow' or 'rolls with the punches'. He has a strong faith in God, and faith God is in control. He is extremely loyal to his friends, and wants to be friends with most all kids. He likes doing things well, and is willing to improve himself.

Something that can be either a strength OR a weakness is Silas' strong sense of right and wrong. His discernment and intuition is a strength, but his indignation over being wronged (or someone else being wronged) can be a weakness when he misunderstands a situation. His feelings run deep.

Another thing that can be either a strength or a weakness is Silas' sociability. He relates well to adults, and can be quite charming, although ornery. He is far from shy, and will engage in conversation with just about anyone. But, because of his visual impairment, he doesn't read body language well, and sometimes infringes on another's personal space. He is improving in this area. One weakness is his use of inappropriate language or words for shock value, or as a way to express anger and resentment.

Loving Silas

June 17, 2014–I share on my facebook wall this quote: "The reality is that you will grieve forever. You will not 'get over' the loss of a loved one; you will learn to live with it. You will heal and you will rebuild yourself around the loss you have suffered. You will be whole again but, you will never be the same. Nor should you be the same, nor would you want to." — Elizabeth Kubler-Ross and John Kessler

I'm angry for Silas. I know he had a wonderful time on his mini "wish" weekend. The only thing I see are his limitations and handicaps appearing in the last six months. It's like he's losing his life one little bit at a time. I'm angry and I'm sad. I want God to change the progression of Silas' life. Am I the only one who can see Silas is slipping away inch by inch?

If I share this, will people doubt my faith? It has nothing to do with faith. I still believe. I believe God can heal Silas right here and now. I believe God is in control. I have to believe God is still God. Immutable. He is still the God Who has healed Silas so many times in his life. He is still the God Who raised His son from the grave so that we also may do so some day. I cling to this.

I am still angry that Silas' physical abilities are compromised more each day, despite exercises. The effects of the treatment are almost worse than the cancer itself.

I keep this to myself. When I cry, I cry by myself. I cry in the shower.

Loving Silas

I have taken many pictures along the way since November 3rd, 2013. As I look back through them, I see a distinct pattern, and it causes me to laugh out loud; severnty-five percent of the photographs are of Silas *eating*.

One of Silas' greatest pleasures is the hunt for good food, and enjoying it with those he loves. His favorite show is "Man vs. Food". His hero is Adam Richman. We had to go to Pappy's the day Blake accompanied us to a clinic visit in St. Louis. We received royal treatment, as if we truly were friends of Adam Richman.

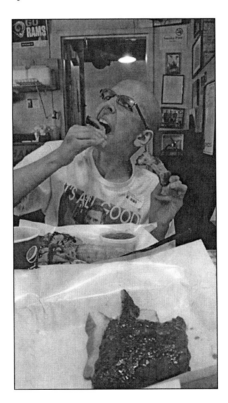

Loving Silas

"I can help someone in lane eight," the cashier shouted. I maneuvered my cart quickly into lane eight. I had several items already on the belt when I realized she was ringing someone up in lane nine. I looked at her quizzically, and she shrugged her shoulders, telling me she'd made a mistake. I went back to my original line, now several places back.

Have you ever stood in line, got all the way to front, and found you were in the wrong line? We sigh, frustrated, and go to the correct line. We might stomp our feet, if only in our minds.

I find it all too easy to get in the wrong line in my spiritual life as well. I see a direction I want to take. I may find Scripture I think supports it. I may even have a friend urging me to move in that direction. I arrive at my "destination" and find I'd been in the wrong line. Things don't work out the way I'd planned. I stomp my feet a little, or throw a full blown fit at God. Why didn't God answer my prayers?

Perhaps my prayers are the problem.

I've prayed many requests. I've prayed many praises. I've prayed prayers of gratitude. Usually about me. All about me, *my* wants, *my* desires, *my* dreams.

Don't get me wrong. God cares about anything I care about. Even the smallest thing, each hair on my head. Am I serving God with that same kind of love? Am I asking God how I can better serve Him and His children? For me, I need to sometimes get out of the way and let someone else ahead of me in line. Sometimes I need to hang back, and wait until God nudges me to move. And, yes, maybe switch lanes.

"For even the Son of Man did not come to be served, but to serve, and to give His life a ransom for many." (Mark 10:45)

"Sitting down, He called the twelve and said to them, 'If anyone wants to be first, he shall be last of all and servant of all.'" (Mark 9:35)

"God, I offer myself to Thee—to build with me and to do with me as Thou wilt. Relieve me of the bondage of self, that I may better do Thy will. Take away my difficulties, that victory over them may bear witness to those I would help of Thy Power, Thy Love, and Thy Way of life. May I do Thy will always!" (3rd Step Prayer, Alcoholics Anonymous)

Silas Living With Cancer

Silas' summers centered around camps. For several years running, he attended camps for "cancer kids," camps for the visually impaired, church retreat camps, and more. In 2009, after a summer full of camps, Silas was in 6th grade. He displayed some strange behaviors that a school nurse finally identified as complex partial seizures. Since he already was an epilepsy patient at SLCH, we started medical tests there.

Silas had week-long videotaped studies of his seizures. His neurologist increased his anti-seizure medication and ordered an additional one. His seizures became still more frequent.

After months of careful consideration and consultations with his full team, Silas had surgery to remove part of his brain. On July 29, 2010, Dr. Limbrick removed Silas' right temporal lobe and hippocampus in a surgery lasting nearly twelve hours.

Prior to the surgery, Silas had one simple request. He wanted to see his brain, and asked his neurosurgeon to take pictures. His request was granted, and we received the pictures by e-mail. By that time, we were part of the growing number of facebook subscribers. Silas insisted on showing the world his "before" and "after" pictures, much to the horror of some.

Silas was in recovery right after his surgery, where I was allowed to speak to him and slowly awaken him. I asked him how he was feeling, and as soon as he could speak, he tried to grin as he told me, "I feel a little light-headed."

Amazingly, Silas was not changed in any discernable way as a result of this surgery. The left side of his brain had already taken over for the damaged right side. Once again, God proved that He is in charge. Period.

Loving Silas

Early August, 2014

Silas' Physical Therapist asks me if I've noticed Silas' left leg being weaker than his right. I have to plead ignorance, since Silas does most of his exercising with Shobi or Keith.

I know. In my inner most being I know. It's back. I say nothing to Silas and I wait. I wait until next session, different therapist. I ask her to assess Silas' legs for asymmetrical strength. She notices, but doesn't know if it's any worse than when Silas started P.T. months ago.

I know. In my inner most being I know. It's back. I say nothing to Silas and I call. I call the Hem Onc clinic to tell them what PT reports. Silas isn't scheduled for an MRI until mid September. He is scheduled for inpatient chemotherapy August 21st. We show up as scheduled. Instead of chemotherapy, Silas is whisked down to radiation for an MRI.

I know. In my inner most being I know what the doctor is going to say before she says it, with tears in her eyes. It's a recurrent PNET tumor. There are no odds. There are no statistics for a sixteen-year-old NF1 patient with a recurrent PNET tumor.

We talk options.

This is no longer my right. From here on, Silas must make all of the decisions. This is Silas' recurrent PNET tumor. This is Silas' brain. This is Silas' life, for as long as he has it.

Silas chooses to have surgery to remove the tumor. His logic is, "You don't know how to fight the enemy unless you know who the enemy is." He wants chemotherapy after surgery. He states, "Even if it doesn't cure my cancer, it may help someone else down the road."

We're allowed to stay overnight at the hospital. That evening, while Silas watches food shows on television, I cry in the shower. He has told me before he wants me to be strong for him. I will not let him see that I know.

I don't know if I can do this.

Loving Silas

September–The Roller Coaster

September 1, 2014

GRATITUDE: So thankful for good insurance. Only twenty-five days into the insurance year, and insurance paid 100% of approved services. I know the state is slow to pay, but thank You, God, for good insurance.

GRATITUDE: So thankful for Silas' positive attitude. Even though he slept most of today, he's adapting, eating, and raring to go tomorrow.

GRATITUDE: So thankful for my salvation, and for Silas' understanding that when his "chemo buddies" or "fellow warriors" lose their battle here on earth, he always, always, says, "Now they are healed."

Silas understands. Silas continues to fight.

September 3, 2014

I drove Silas down to St. Louis Children's Hospital last night late after consulting with Hem Onc on-call doctors. Silas has been so sleepy the last couple days, and in so much ear and head pain. I don't know if it's post-herpetic like left over from the shingles he had in March or from the brain tumor. The doctors are bewildered at why the post-herpetic pain would flare up again. In the past, it only happened after chemotherapy. They increase Silas' IV pain medication and all of his at-home meds. It works for three or four hours at a time. He also has vomited a few times since being here. They aren't sure why. We feel the prayers especially right now, as he dozes peacefully, no wincing at all.

September 4, 2014

Thank you to everyone waiting for a post from us. We covet your prayers more than ever now. Surgery has been cancelled for next week. The tumor is in a precarious place, and after deliberation, his team of doctors has said surgery is not an option.

Next step is to have a lumbar puncture, while we are here as in-patient. If there are cancer cells in the spinal fluid, they will proceed immediately to aggressive chemotherapy. If there are no cancer cells in the spinal fluid, they will investigate to see if Gamma Knife Radiation is an option for immediate attention to the new tumor. Silas would have his Radiology Doctor from last winter, Dr. Perkins, to tend to this.

We pray for wisdom. We pray for pain-free days. We pray for God's Healing.

September 5, 2014

Thank You, God, we were here and not home when his unrelenting pain hit. That this caused all of the teams' ears to perk up and re-examine Silas' medical history. Thank You, Lord, we are in such a wonderful place. We have such a successful relationship with the doctors here. Let us, please, God, rest in what You have in store for Silas. Let me be the hands and feet of Jesus as I serve You, through serving Silas every day. In Jesus' name, Amen.

September 6, 2014

Morning–Silas' fever is down a bit (Thank You, God.) His other symptoms—fatigue, vomiting, general malaise—are now being attributed to pressure in the brain due to the new and fast growing brain tumor. Hem Onc is talking about a new medication to combat that. Silas responds best to me reading out loud to him. He actually perks up.

Afternoon–One of the doctors told us they are planning Gamma Knife on the same day Silas' surgery was cancelled, September 10. We will be here until then. Inpatient chemotherapy will follow. I know I see the asymmetry distinctly and I do not want to wait until the end of the month like they were discussing yesterday.

September 7, 2014

Today was like yesterday until the CT scan. Silas has a brain bleed and he's being rushed to PICU. I'm calling close friends to post updates and mobilize prayer warriors. Another CT scan shows the bleed has stabilized.

September 8, 2014

Silas is coming back from an MRI. We're still in the PICU for the brain bleed. Neurosurgery is still looking at Wednesday for surgery to relieve pressure. They may not be able to do anything with the tumor. We have believers all around us. A former roommate's mom came by, and asked me if I ever sing, based on hearing my speaking voice. God gave me a smile.

Silas is having lots of head pain, and I'm not sure what's going on. Childlife Services brought Silas his own stuffed dog because the Touch Team can't visit him here in the PICU.

September 9, 2014

Silas' head pain is relentless. Please pray now! Thank you. I've never seen him hold his head like this.

Surgery is scheduled for tomorrow to relieve the pressure from the bleeding, and to get as much of the tumor as possible. Doctors have advised us Silas might not make it through surgery, or it could leave him with total left-side paralysis. They asked me to talk with Silas about advanced directives. How do I talk to my child about that?

Silas told me he understands, and he made sure I understand there's only one thing he's concerned about. If he doesn't make it, I'm to be sure his brain goes to Dr. Rubin's lab for brain tumor research. I feel numb inside.

September 10, 2014

Afternoon–Doctor came in to talk after surgery. It went well. While vacating the brain bleed, they were able to remove most of the tumor, which is better than expected. They won't know anything about motor function until after he wakes up. God is so good. Keep the prayers for healing and recovery coming.

Evening–Silas is doing extremely well. The movement he is able to do on the left side is better than anticipated. A quote from his doctor, "We would expect nothing less from Silas." He will experience a lot of head and facial swelling over the next 72 hours which is normal for this type of surgery.

Silas Living With Cancer

Silas required physical therapy after his lobectomy, although the surgery didn't seem to have affected any of his other skills, motor or otherwise. One of the physical therapists worked with the local chapter of AMBUCS to get a tricycle for Silas. This was no ordinary tricycle. It was a full sized adult trike, with a basket in the back and a bell on the handle bars. The line of thinking was to get Silas moving. Like many people with vision impairment, Silas didn't always get enough exercise.

Because of Silas' visual impairment, Silas learned to use a white cane for mobility. It became his eyes, essentially "seeing" the surface ahead of him, making him aware of changes in terrain and more.

Silas was unable to use his white cane when he was riding his tricycle. When Silas rode his tricycle, he was unable to see the road ahead of him. Whenever he rode, an adult needed to accompany Silas, describing aloud what was ahead, and warning him of approaching dangers.

Silas was strong, and could pedal fast. His dad's legs didn't always move as quickly as Silas could pedal. The inevitable happened when Silas barreled down a sidewalk which ended with steps down to the street. Thank goodness for the helmet that came with his trike!

Silas was up in no time, but didn't show enthusiasm for riding after that. He may even have walked the trike home that day without a white cane.

Loving Silas

September 11, 2014

My sweet friend and youth pastor's wife, Sarah helped keep our troops informed:

"I know that I've been flooding your News Feeds with updates on Silas, but I have to share one more time. Gloria just called me to tell me that Silas is now on the 12th floor (out of PICU), has been taken off of his restricted diet and sent his mother on a food run for chili. Um, what? This kid had brain surgery 24 hours ago! The doctors can't be sure yet, but they THINK they got all of the tumor and said that they were able to stop all of the hemorrhaging which means that it's possible Silas will be able to leave the hospital feeling stronger than when he got there. Gloria thinks they may be able to go home on Sunday, Monday at the latest. Gloria sounds great, but is asking for prayers for "boot camp" which starts tomorrow. She'll need to start working with Silas on stretches and getting his braces back on. Pray for Gloria to have patience and strength to help him and pray for Silas to not be too annoyed with his mom."

I posted later in the day: This is the first time I've had time to get on the laptop in days. Silas is doing *fantastic*. He has a long way to go to get his legs back under him. I was unsuccessful in finding chili, but found his usual breakfast fare of taquitos and breakfast burritos to heat in the microwave. The cafeteria here is under construction, so they don't even have soup.

I can't begin to express how encouraged I am by God's timing. If Silas hadn't had that brain bleed, they wouldn't have gone in to do surgery at all. They got most of the tumor, too. A week ago, it looked pretty hopeless. Now we're gearing up for the next step and I do mean "step." Steps! Steps! We have to get this boy walking. He has lost *no* function noticeable yet and I'm getting ready to stretch his ankles. He is not going to like me within a couple of days, but he will work, as he always has, to regain whatever strength he can. Thank you all for your prayers, and if anyone wants to bring Silas chili, we're on the 12th floor, room 20B. (He also loves big burgers.)
Praise God!

Loving Silas

Silas was released from the hospital on the evening of September 17th. He was to report for chemotherapy the next morning, so he and I stayed at a nearby hotel. I told him he could have whatever he wanted from room service. He had two orders of escargot and filet mignon. He was in heaven.

The next morning, Silas' dad picked us up and we headed to the Hem Onc clinic at SLCH for outpatient chemo. Silas had to be checked out first by his doctor. Silas' dad stepped out for coffee. As soon as Silas and I were in the examining room, Silas started listing to one side, and his face started contorting. I remember screaming for help.

The next few hours are a blur. We were busy every minute with medical staff. Silas was admitted to PICU, after the MRI which diagnosed he had experienced a stroke. He was fully immobile on his left side.

Loving Silas

"You may have to fight a battle more than once to win it." (Margaret Thatcher)

I thought of Silas immediately when I read this. I can't begin to count how many times he fought the battle with brain tumors... seizures... brain surgeries... narcolepsy... epilepsy... side effects of chemotherapy... stroke.

God's idea of victory is often different than ours. Praise Jesus we can have the ultimate victory through Him.

Loving Silas

September 19, 2014

This is the first time I've not had doctors bothering both of us. Brock is here. He gave me some relief so I could sleep three full hours.

Silas is showing a tiny bit of improvement on his left side. The stroke happened in the tumor bed. It was the major artery the tumor had been around.

Thank you all for your prayers and love.

Silas says he is healed–this side or the other.

We both know. We don't talk about it. I cry in the shower.

Silas Living With Cancer

The entire time Silas went to St. Louis Children's Hospital, he looked forward to the visits. The hospital is so kid friendly, bright and colorful, with clown docs visiting, and a Childlife Services department distracting young patients from the pain and gravity of their situations. Whenever we visited, Silas looked forward most to the Touch Team, a group of therapy dogs who visit patients in their rooms, some even providing snuggles. If you knew Silas, you know he loved dogs. No matter how he felt, the Touch Team made his day.

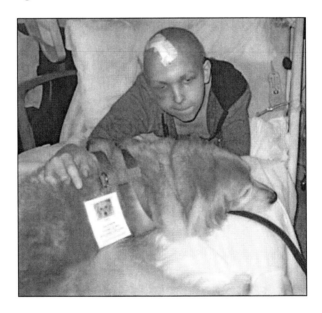

Loving Silas

September 21, 2014

My friend Sarah posted on facebook for us. "Latest update on Silas: I spoke to Gloria. Silas has recovered a lot of motion in his left leg and some in his shoulder. His left arm and hand are still immobile post-stroke. They are wanting to do another CT scan to make sure there is no bleeding, but the neurosurgeon sounded encouraging. Everyone is tired, but trying to stay positive. Please keep praying for God's clear direction for the family and doctors."

Within hours, I had to post as well. "Thank you, Sarah, for posting for us this morning. We've had many changes since then, not in a forward direction. Silas has lost mobility in his left leg, became lethargic, and is slurring his speech. Another CT this afternoon showed no change from this morning, but neurosurgery is concerned about pressure on the brain. If he stays the same overnight, they will take him to the O.R. to insert a tiny tube to weigh the pressure in his brain. If that is the problem, they will insert a shunt. I was told the goal is to get him home as soon as possible. I'm not sure what this means as far as any upcoming chemotherapy. We received a denial from insurance covering at least part of the chemo, saying it wasn't protocol for his type of tumor. Brock and I are switching off at his bedside, since we have the tiny side of the hospital room. Please pray for Silas' brother, Shobi, too, as he has several papers due this week at college. Thank you all for all you've done for us."

Later still I updated, because so many people were inquiring. "Thank you for all the prayers as we enter the night's sleep. Silas won't sleep much with hourly neuro checks and vitals. He tried so hard to swallow water earlier after we bathed him, but the awesome nurses aren't comfortable with him swallowing pills again, so we're back to IV meds exclusively. Nothing by mouth after midnight, and neurosurgery will decide in the morning if Silas will have surgery or not, based on his night."

Loving Silas

September 22, 2014

Praise God! No hydrocephalus. The doctor finished about a half hour ago. Silas is in recovery with a drain on the left side of his head. The drain is intended to be there about a day. He'll be in PICU for that time. After that, Silas will go back into "boot camp" to relearn how to swallow, walk, teach his left leg and arm to move again, and hopefully start chemotherapy late this week. Thank you *all* for all of your prayers.

Silas Living With Cancer

Silas was a typical teenager with typical hopes and dreams. His passion for video games combined beautifully with his visual impairment in his career choice. He wanted to design video games for the visually impaired. He wanted to put Braille characters on the controllers to help identify the buttons. He wanted to improve the graphics. These were only some of his ideas.

He also described what would be the perfect person to be his wife someday. She had to know how to drive, because he never would be able to. She had to accept the fact he most likely could not father children biologically, due to all of the cancer treatments he'd had in his life. She had to love animals, especially large dogs. She either had to love to cook or love to eat out, or both. Lastly, in Silas' words, "She has to be hot."

Loving Silas

September 23, 2014

Some good things to remember: Christ convicts, Satan condemns. Christ chooses, Satan captures. Christ compels, Satan constricts. Christ clarifies, and Satan confuses.

Thank you to a dear friend from Decatur who surprised me today. We prayed, laughed, cried, and laughed some more. It feels so good to share some time with someone from back home.

Tonight, I've slept awhile. I woke up with praises in my head and Silas asking for me. I worked his left hand and wrist for a while, and the cold feeling left. He said he could feel me kiss his fingers. He has some sensation in that arm, but no movement. Yesterday, the doctors said his leg will come back faster than his arm. I love the conversations Silas and I have while we're doing things like his stretches.

We had a visit from our favorite Chaplain here, and we sang over Silas, "Walking and Leaping and Praising God." Silas says he wants to walk again and we are so ready to work for it. I'm going back to sleep. With a grateful heart.

Loving Silas

This has been an exciting, confusing day. Silas was released from PICU after removing his External Ventricle Drain, from which they pulled some spinal fluid. They will know in a few days if there are new cancer cells in that fluid.

We have the most amazing medical team. At the *exact* moment the neurosurgeon started the procedure, the Childlife Specialist walked up behind me and asked Silas to play Twenty Questions. This distracted Silas a tiny bit from the numbing needle. However, when the nurse went to remove the arterial line from his wrist, Silas pinched her, hard! What a stinker.

Silas hasn't had anything at all to eat or drink for about five days, due to the left side weakness and NPO orders. He has to learn to swallow and speak clearly again. Speech Therapy came to the rescue. Within a couple of hours, Silas was eating chocolate pudding and macaroni and cheese. He's on soft foods only, so he asked if they could put a steak in the blender. When the speech therapist asked him to swallow hard, as if swallowing a golf ball, he looked up, seriously, and asked, "Did you ever swallow a golf ball?" The whole room burst out laughing.

Silas cannot use his left arm at all yet, and left leg barely. The neurologist's assessment when we moved into twelfth floor reports he can distinguish a line right down the middle of Silas' chest where the sensation of pain stops on the left. We have a long hard road. We don't know anything beyond this moment. Silas says if he can help anyone else, he wants to proceed with chemotherapy. Insurance is denying the third in the series of four drugs, Thalidomide. Dr. King is pulling hard for it. Thalidomide is one of the drugs Silas took, way back in 2006-2007. That protocol finally kicked his first tumors' butts. He asked me to sing to him, and closed his eyes. I sang, but all I could think of was when he was little. He would yell, "No, Mommy," when I sang in the daytime, because he thought he had to go to bed.

The Neurosurgery team was here. They are so pleased with his attitude, and provided the healing continues, his chemotherapy will start on Friday.

Please pray specifically:

1. Silas does as well with this chemotherapy as he has always done in the past.
2. Insurance will approve the entire protocol for a recurrent PNET tumor.
3. We will be allowed to stay on this floor where we are so comfortable.

More importantly, please pray God's will be done and that we all have Silas' attitude about how *big* God is.

Silas Living With Cancer

When Silas' dad and I separated years ago, we spoke to both boys apart from each other. Silas was very quiet when he heard the news. When I asked him to talk to me, to tell me what his thoughts were, he told me, "Mom, I'm just a bobber on the water. I go with the flow."

No words could have captured the essence of Silas better. No matter how bad the circumstances, Silas never stayed upset long. He was resilient. He never let things get to him. Not his parents' broken marriage. Not cancer.

Silas' lead physician, Dr. Allison King spoke often of her desire to have more of Silas' laid back "bobber" attitude. That outlook served him so well.

Loving Silas

September 26, 2014

Speech Therapy taught Silas how to swallow, then he graduated to soft foods. Hunger is a great motivator, especially for Silas. Now that he's on to all foods, he's eating everything in sight. One of our most loved doctors was in, watching Silas get up from bed. He said our main neurosurgeon spoke in conference yesterday about Silas, and voiced that he strongly believes Silas will walk again. *Praise God!* You should see how hard Silas is working. He finally got to sit up in the wheel chair, look out the window, and eat some of a burger.

Silas has been approved for the program here for recovery from his stroke, so we will be here at least six weeks, up to three months. He starts chemotherapy today as well, so we have two new journeys starting. He is working hard in physical, occupational, and speech therapies, twice daily. His wit and humor keep the staff laughing.

He doesn't have much time to watch TV, but American Pickers on the History Channel and the food programs are his favorites. Silas enjoys me reading aloud to him, so we've been reading "America the Edible" by his hero, Adam Richman.

Silas would love visitors, as would I, anytime.

Loving Silas

October 5, 2014

We pray before every meal, and Silas always asks God to bless all those who are suffering. We are getting settled in to living here at St. Louis Children's Hospital for a month or more. Silas is doing well at using his 'good' arm to grab his 'bad' arm, and move himself around.

Silas had surgery this morning to put a shunt in. This will reduce the pressure in his brain, and let any fluid drain to his abdomen. He and I both slept most afternoon, after a wonderful visit from my friends Phyllis and Leah. They brought pictures of new puppies who are back home in Decatur. His eyes opened wide when Phyllis showed him. Silas is in the Neuro Rehab program, which means lots of therapies twice a day plus visits from the School Room here. He's pooped today, but normally is so willing to work. When he got back from surgery, he told the doctors his head feels better already.

I got into some trouble last night. I fell and cracked my head on the floor so I had my own trip to the ER after lots of bleeding. Yes, a concussion. Yes, staples to close. But I got back to Silas' room about midnight last night. I got a shower and shampooed, and I've ordered food for Silas. He isn't focused on any one food so a variety is coming up. Thank you all for your prayers and love, and I promise to be better with the updates. I definitely went into "hiding" for a couple of days. Please know how much we appreciate all of you.

I have not been listening to friends and family who tell me, "Take care of yourself." I don't even know what that means. I manage to grab food here and there, and I sleep like a log. My fear has overtaken my faith at times, and my anxiety is running rampant.

Loving Silas

October 6, 2014

I am checking myself into detox this afternoon. Silas is in good hands with the nursing staff. I hope to be out in a few days. Silas needs visitors. I can't do this by myself. I know because I've tried doing exactly that here. I'm being honest and laying it out there. I will not be in touch by laptop or phone for a few days.

October 10, 2014

I was discharged today from the rehab hospital, feeling recharged and re-equipped with many tools I hadn't been using to cope with this stressful situation. At SLCH, we met with the Neuro Rehab staff, about twelve medical personnel, to discuss Silas and what's been happening with him. He continues to receive a lot of therapies, but has been so tired. He hasn't made much physical progress, except to strengthen his left leg. He still cannot stand, but both his dad and I have been learning how to transfer him from bed to wheelchair and back. Silas is one big kid. His sharp wit and wry sense of humor are still there. It looks like another seven weeks or so in the Neuro Rehab program. It was reported in the meeting that he has become a master at the game of Taboo. I'm so glad they make his therapy fun.

The dietician ordered that steak for Silas last night, although she wouldn't deliver it rare. I understand from Brock that Silas groaned at having to eat a medium-cooked steak. Brock and he both had a rough night, due to Silas' severe nerve pain around his right ear. He got short term relief from pain meds, and they increased his Neurontin. We're praying for the best. Please pray for relief from the pain, so he can be more alert without his pain meds.

Silas Living With Cancer

Silas and Shobi have had a pretty typical relationship as brothers. Sibling rivalry didn't last too long at any given stretch. Silas looked up to his older brother, and Shobi looked out for his younger brother.

During the years Silas was in remission before his lobectomy, the boys seemed to always be pestering each other. Each blamed the other one for everything.

One night I got up to investigate a noise and found Silas in the kitchen. His sleep-wake cycle never did totally approach normal, so finding him there was not all that unusual. A glass of orange juice was on the counter.

I told Silas he needed to go back to bed and at least try to sleep. Silas took a couple of steps upward. Being thirsty, I quickly drank the orange juice.

Silas began to softly cry. I asked him what was wrong, and he answered through his tears, "The orange juice." I assured him he could have another glass in the morning.

Silas took a few more steps upward, and started crying more loudly, saying, "It was Shobi's." As I ushered him into his room and bed, I once again tried to comfort him with a promise of more orange juice in the morning. Silas was sobbing by now.

As I tucked him in, he was beside himself. Suddenly he gasped between cries, "I peed in it!"

I have never ran so quickly to the bathroom in my life. That orange juice came back up of it's own volition.

Upon further investigation, Silas confessed he was getting even with his older brother. Silas had been blamed for something Shobi had done, or Shobi didn't get punished for something Silas thought he should have been. I don't know for certain, except to say Silas felt some injustice had been done to him, and Shobi should pay.

To this day, I don't know whether to laugh or cry, but it's one of my favorite Silas stories.

Loving Silas

October 13, 2014

I dropped off Shobi at the hospital early this morning, to spend the day with Silas and their dad. We had talked about the effects of the stroke, but Shobi wasn't prepared. He said later that the hardest part was seeing Silas in such pain on the right side of his head and right ear. The pain management team has talked about possibly cauterizing the nerve feeding that ear, in hopes Silas would be able to go without all the heavy duty medicines they have him on. The meds tire him and slur his speech even more than the stroke did. They did have a good visit, between Silas' therapies. Shobi delivered Silas' new iPad and set it up for him. Shobi and I arrived back in Decatur about 8pm tonight.

I have not been allowed to see Silas, even to visit him supervised, since Monday, October 6th. I will continue doing the right thing, putting one foot in front of the other, trusting our sovereign God. My outpatient rehab went well this morning, and I look forward to going Monday, Wednesday, and Friday for a few weeks, west of St. Louis Children's Hospital. I am learning and re-learning much. I'm home right now, getting laundry done and sweeping the leaves out of the kitchen. I'm looking forward to a home group AA meeting in the morning. I am so grateful the tornado skipped over this part of town.

Thank you all for your continued prayers.

Loving Silas

October 14, 2014

I've had some private message inquiries, and I guess I have been a little vague about the activities the past couple of weeks. So, since I am only as sick as my secrets, and because getting it "out there" keeps me more accountable, I am posting a very candid account here now.

I am a recovering alcoholic. I have had sixteen years sobriety, then three years, then two years, with relapses in between. While at the hospital with Silas this fall, I relapsed again, trying to self medicate. I had no idea I was Bipolar, which was diagnosed at the rehab facility during detox early this month. I am so thankful I went, as they put me on the correct meds, and I am feeling much better, with no desire to drink.

The point I am trying to make is this. Had I been on the correct meds, I most likely would not have reached for wine to handle the stress. The hospital is saying I am a risk, and I understand. Last week, when I told them I would gladly go to an outpatient program in St. Louis, the medical staff said I could return to Silas' side, while attending the program eight miles west of the hospital.

SLCH Risk Management team has a different opinion, and won't let me see Silas at all, even supervised. So, I am driving 143 miles, one way, three days a week, to attend the outpatient program for dual diagnosis/alcohol dependence. Silas tells me on the phone that he wants me with him so badly, and my heart aches because I can't be there. We may have some intervention from our DCFS Case Manager, who believes I am doing the right things, but I don't know when that relief will come. In the mean time, I have enjoyed some quality time with Silas' brother, Shobi, and got a lot done here at home.

I am taking responsibility for my disease(s), and will continue to focus on recovery, by the Grace of God, whether I am allowed to see my son or not.

I appreciate any and all prayers for Silas, and for me. Thank you.

Silas Living With Cancer

Silas and I spent a lot of time in the car over the years. His first MRI was at St. Louis Children's Hospital. We never went anywhere else after that to treat Silas' brain tumors. At his annual Hematology-Oncology appointment in spring of 2013, they didn't schedule an annual checkup for 2014. Silas had enjoyed a time of remission from all physical attacks. So instead of an annual exam, Silas was scheduled for the "Late Effects Clinic" for 2014. There, a team would meet with Silas to be sure he understood how to live with the real and possible side effects of all the chemotherapy, and years of imaging and scans he had endured, and of the cancer itself. He also would start planning a future which included fellowship with other teens, survivors of cancer. When November 2013, brought a new brain tumor, it brought the worst, and it forever changed our lives.

It was in the car that November that Silas and I started talking a lot about God. He had asked to be baptized in 2010 at Northwest Christian Church, prior to the surgery to remove roughly a fourth of his brain. But now was different. He was older. He had a deeper understanding of God. And, suddenly, in the midst of our conversation about faith and God, he had been overwhelmed with humility. Through tears, he confessed, "I know I'm saved, but I just don't understand why God would save me." I have had discussions with adults about this, but I felt so inadequate to face such a task with my son. I was truly humbled God allowed me that defining moment.

That moment was defining in other ways. It was a moment in which Silas and I both had our guard down. We both knew this tumor was so rare that only three others in medical history had his exact set of circumstances. We both knew what Silas was facing. In that moment, Silas decided he was "all in". Silas made all decisions about treatment after that. I was his mouthpiece, his advocate. I gave him multiple opportunities to stop treatment over the next year. He always said forging ahead with treatment would help others through research even if it didn't save his life. He never questioned his salvation after that day.

Silas knew he was saved, and he knew why and how and by Whom. Even if God chose to heal him on the "other side," Silas knew our God is bigger than the odds.

Are you prepared to have such a discussion when the opportunity arises? Because it will.

"For the grace of God that brings salvation has appeared to all men, teaching us that, denying ungodliness and worldly lusts, we should live soberly, righteously, and godly in the present age, looking for the blessed hope and glorious appearing of our great God and Savior Jesus Christ, who gave Himself for us, that He might redeem us from every lawless deed and purify for Himself His own special people, zealous for good works." (Titus 2:11-14)

Loving Silas

October 16, 2014

Reading my Bible this morning, I came across some old sermon notes, "Jesus asleep in the boat is greater than any storm in your life." I challenge you to think on that one.

October 18, 2014

Silas had a boat load of visitors from Decatur Christian School today. They brought several cards and Silas wanted to read every single letter. I don't know what was more important, the hugs or the smiles they brought with them. Everyone gathered around and prayed over Silas. Silas asked prayer warriors to ask God to restore his mobility in his left arm and leg. What a wonderful group of kids.

Silas misses them all. The hugs from each one has renewed his strength and his commitment to work hard at his therapies.

Decatur Christian School has supported Silas from before the start of this journey. He enrolled there for his Sophomore year, and was immediately embraced as the incredible, independent person he is. The fundraising and generosity of a group of kids has been beyond what we ever could have imagined. We have a family at DCS.

Loving Silas

October 19, 2014

God reminded me today how much he loves me. At church, it was as if he spoke right to me. I've been having a hard time forgiving myself. Today's sermon at church was all about forgiveness.

I was reminded God is a sovereign God. No matter the circumstance, God is in control. Whether he allowed it or caused it, God is in control. If I continue to believe my actions are who I am, I am giving that belief power to ruin my life, and I cannot forgive myself. When I finally understood what was being said, I could accept responsibility, I could accept my part, and I could forgive myself and move on.

I was reminded this Scripture applies to me, and is about me: "Be kind to one another, tender-hearted, forgiving each other, just as God in Christ also has forgiven you." (Ephesians 4:32)

I had a wonderful visit tonight with Silas. I am now allowed to visit for a couple of hours at a time, with supervision from a friend of my choosing. He asked me to read from Adam Richman's book "America the Edible." What an interesting read.

I had delivered escargot from the restaurant at the hotel where I'm staying tonight. He ate two servings plus chocolate chip cookies, compliments of the front desk manager, who loves Silas. (This is the hotel where we stayed for his mini "wish" weekend in June.)

Then, Silas told me he misses me holding him, and asked me to crawl in bed next to him to read. When I did, I noticed his hair is falling out again, especially in the back, all over his pillow case. It had grown back in a bit darker, so it's evident. I loved cuddling with him as he reached for my hand constantly, and seeing him laugh and smile at some of the antics in that book. Thank you, Maggie, for accompanying me, making this visit possible.

Silas will start another daily oral chemo drug tomorrow, Thalidomide, which can cause more neuropathy. Please pray against side effects. His next "5-day round" will start October 24th. Thank you all for your prayers and loving support.

Loving Silas

October 21, 2014

The dentist put my permanent crown on this morning, I saw my counselor, and I got a phone call from the hospital I'm "good to go". Explanation: I am being restored to Silas' bedside as his primary caretaker!

I will still go to Outpatient Treatment down there Monday-Wednesday-Friday, and I will attend Celebrate Recovery and AA meetings. But I will be able to stay with Silas, read to him, help him bathe, and sleep in the pull-out bed at his side. I am so excited, so thankful. Because I am on unpaid leave, Brock will go back home and work, even getting overtime, to make up for my lack of income. Thank you all for your prayers and support. I will continue to need visitors for both of us. I will need friends to stay with Silas in the evenings as I go to meetings two or three times each week.

Loving Silas

October 22, 2014

I am so thankful Silas is sitting up and *wants* to sit up. He is so alert this week compared to last, and he is participating well in his therapies, not just letting it happen to him. I'm off to my Outpatient Treatment this morning, and he has already chosen what he wants the nurses to get him for lunch while I'm gone. He is rolling with the punches, and we are enjoying each other's company so much. Thank you all for your prayers and love and support.

In my readings today, I read Psalm 100 to Silas, and I have LOTS of notes in the margins from my pastor's sermons:

God gives good gifts in the midst of trials (I'll say);

Give thanks in all things–this is not circumstantial;

We should have at least 3 thankful responses to God's blessings: 1–Shout 2–SING 3–Bend Knees & Raise Hands!

I'm all for this today. Please, Lord, help me keep this attitude always.

Loving Silas

October 23, 2014

Awesome readings today in my Bible and meditation books. I'm thankful I write in the margins when I take sermon notes. I usually note who the preacher was as well, which helps me remember and hear it again. Today, I came across three jots in a row, where I'd noted Scott Monette was the source. These weren't simply "feel good" notations. These were uncomfortable. These were some good instructions for life. I'm grateful for Northwest Christian Church and our pastors there.

October is Pastor Appreciation month, so I want to express how grateful I am for ours. Our family at NWCC is truly blessed to be shepherded by such devoted pastors. Sometimes when we're quietly talking, Silas will remember and tell me something from one of Pastor Steve's sermons, and that blesses my heart so much.

Super Silas will move to 9th floor Friday for five days of chemotherapy, then be discharged. He will be sent to a long term pediatric rehab and convalescence facility called Ranken Jordan which is about twelve miles west of SLCH. We've been told it is a fantastic place, with all the focus on rehabilitative therapies. This is a bridge from the acute hospital setting to going home. It is closer to the Outpatient Treatment facility where I go Monday-Wednesday-Friday. I am still trying to process it all. Silas just "goes with the flow". We love, trust and respect the staff here. They believe this is a good move for Silas.

Loving Silas

October 24, 2014

Dear Silas,

You are not the same as when you checked into the hospital in so much pain September 3, 2014.

You are not the same as when you were first diagnosed with brain tumors in 2004.

It has been a roller coaster ride from hell. And I hate that I cannot change it. I can't protect you from the approaching storm.

I know that, short of a miracle, you will not survive this second PNET tumor.

I don't know when, I don't know the details of how, but I know this one will rob you of life.

I hate it for that.

Already, this thing has taken on a life of its own. It has stolen your mobility.

This cancer and the stroke it caused has stolen your smile. It has left you with only one half of that amazing grin!

I admire you, Silas. Your will to fight this foe to the bitter end.

I admire you, Silas. Your acceptance of depending on others for nearly everything, even to the point of wearing a diaper.

I admire you, Silas. Your lack of fear. For I am afraid. I am afraid of life without you. I know that is coming.

I am afraid of what to do with myself after you are gone. Taking care of you is my life right now.

It is an honor and a privilege. It is a humbling experience. It is a frustrating responsibility. I hate pushing you to do more when you are exhausted. I hate that you will be leaving the hospital to go to a long term facility soon.

This hospital has become our home. Our safe haven. This hospital has been our friend since your original brain tumor diagnosis over ten years ago. Your doctors have become our family. I love them and trust them. I am afraid of life without them as well.

Please forgive me for jumping the gun. I know you are not gone yet. But I see a tiny bit of you slip away every so often. And each time that happens, grief grabs my heart, tears me apart.

I wish I had a timeline. I wish I knew exactly how long we still have together here on earth.

I wish I had your acceptance. I wish I had your lack of fear. I wish I could "go with the flow" like you do.

Today, I will take your lead.

You are being moved to hem onc floor for chemotherapy, before being discharged to the other, as yet unseen, facility.

I will act "as if" I am flexible. I will act "as if" I am rolling with the punches. I will trust God to hold my hand and walk me through this.

I will hold your hand, Silas. I will hold you. I will tell you it will all work out. I will tell you I believe this. I do believe it will all work out, just not the way I want it to.

I will be your human rock to lean on. I believe God will give me that strength I need to support you as you travel this strange path.

I love you, my baby.

You have made my life so much better.

Thank you for making me a better person.

Love,

Mom

Loving Silas

October 26, 2014

In the margins of my Bible today, I found notes from a sermon dated 6-6-10. Silas and I talk every day about what I'm reading in Scripture, so this day is no different.

Why do bad things happen to good people?

We can ask Why? Where is God?

He is always always here.

We have to accept we live in a fallen and broken world. Period.

Even if God causes or allows it, pain is never, ever, for naught.

Read Romans 8:28. If we understand this, and look, we have an amazing opportunity to see God at work.

This is so true of Silas' entire life. When I look at the way he has touched lives, when I look at his attitude through it all, when I see him walk out of here repeatedly only three days after brain surgeries, when I try to count all the amazing people we've met because he is where he is, when I read the notes of encouragement, love, and support, I. SEE. GOD. AT. WORK.

Loving Silas

October 27, 2014

Silas was hungry for candy earlier, specifically, the chocolate mix which has four different kinds of candy bars. I picked some up. He ate one of each kind out of our bowl, then started offering some to any nurse or tech entering his room. Then, he asked his nurse to take it around to do some reverse trick or treating, to share the candy with the other patients here, as well as the nurses. He is the sweetest kid.

October 28, 2014

I don't know that I've ever been so frightened. Silas had a seizure and became totally unresponsive. The staff on the floor flooded into the room, and suddenly we were in Intensive Care. There's no telling what caused it at this point. It could be brain bleed, it could be tumor bed activity.

October 29, 2014

I've had a CD playing over and over for hours now in the PICU. It's the CD I played during both Silas' and Shobi's births. I keep hearing, "On Christ the Solid Rock I stand. All other ground is sinking sand." and "I'm amazed, at all you've done for me." This has helped us keep our focus on the Sovereign God Who is in control of all of this. God knows the big plan so I don't have to know.

Silas still claims "his" song, by Matt Vollmer & the Great Romance, "Bigger Than the Odds".

October 30, 2014

Silas awoke about 2am screaming in pain from the outside of his right ear and the back of his head. We were up for a few hours until the pain was under control. By this afternoon, the pain is managed by medication and body language. As soon as he starts grabbing his ear and applying pressure, the nurses know it's flaring up again.

Silas was moved back to 9th floor after another CT was done, which showed no change since Tuesday night's CT. The brain bleed could have been from a few days earlier. It is a relatively small bleed, and there is room for more bleeding where the tumor was resected September 10.

Neurosurgery says the bleed was most likely caused by new tumor growth, since it is right where the old tumor was. We've known all along that, short of a miracle, there probably will be recurrent tumors in that area. This explains why Silas' chemotherapy is so aggressive.

Silas continues to tell me, "I'm healed. This side or the other."

Loving Silas

November 2, 2014

This weekend has been emotional for me. It was exactly a year ago Silas awoke in the middle of the night, holding his head in pain and vomiting. This year has been a journey, and I've wanted to hide a few times. We couldn't have gotten through without God and all of you holding us up in prayer, with love. Thank you for all your support. We can never find the words to tell you how much we appreciate it. God Bless you all.

Stand By Silas posted on their facebook page:

"For I know the plans I have for you," declares The Lord. "plans to prosper you and not to harm you, plans to give you hope and a future." (Jeremiah 29:11)

Silas wanted us to share that with everyone standing by him. God has a plan for each and every one of us, and though we might not think it's the right way, He knows what He's doing.

Silas Living With Cancer

Silas has used a white cane for mobility since he was in first grade. With his level of vision impairment, he has difficulty with depth perception, steps and such. However, if he is in familiar surroundings, he is known for conveniently "forgetting" where he parked his cane.

He wants to be like everyone else. But he's not. Nobody is like Silas.

At Halloween a while back, we were heading out the door to church, where we serve the community by providing a Trunk-and-Treat event. Costumes are welcome, and Silas insisted he had his on. We all laughed together when he declared, "I'm going as a blind man."

Loving Silas

November 10, 2014

Today is the big day! Silas will move to Ranken Jordan Pediatric Bridge Hospital, a bridge between the hospital and home.

When Silas wakes in the mornings, I usually share the Scripture I've read each day. Today is Psalm 27. The page is covered with sermon notes about truly seeking God and how that is true worship. I am so blessed with awesome pastors.

Here are a few thoughts for today as well, "Meditation For the Day–One thing I do, forgetting those things which are behind, and reaching forth unto those things that are before, I press onward toward the goal." We should forget those things which are behind us and press onward toward something better. We can believe that God has forgiven us for all our past sins, provided we are honestly trying to live today the way we believe He wants us to live. We can wipe clean the slate of the past. We can start today with a clean slate and go forward with confidence toward the goal that has been set before us.

Prayer for the Day–I pray that I may drop off the load of the past. I pray that I may start today with a light heart and a new confidence."

That truly is my prayer for today, as we start another leg in Silas' journey.

May God richly bless you all for your prayers and continuing support of this precious child of God.

Loving Silas

November 19, 2014

Silas is scheduled for 5 days of in-patient chemotherapy every four weeks, as long as his blood counts hold strong, which they are doing right now. We're leaving Ranken Jordan for 11:30 am appointment at St. Louis Children's Hospital with Dr. King, then admission to 9th floor. We will return here after five days of chemo. Silas has the best attitude about it all–and has worked extra hard today in OT and Speech Therapy.

He wanted to go back to the therapy pool one more time. The other day when he was in there, it was amazing. With the weights and floats, Silas was actually walking! Silas was elated. True, it took two therapists to manage it, but Silas was walking.

He enjoys pulling a scripture a day out of his "TRUST GOD" Super Silas jar on his bedside table. If we don't do it, he gets on me to do it. I love this boy to pieces. Thank you all for your prayers.

Loving Silas

November 21, 2014

What an honor and what a fun "field trip". Since we're right next door, Silas and I were able to visit Dr. Josh Rubin, research scientist, at his laboratory. Many years ago, Dr. Rubin was one of Silas' original Hematology Oncology doctors. Silas got a tour of the lab, and he was able to view brain cancer cells under the microscope. He actually identified the different parts of the microscope, thanks to what he has learned from his biology teacher at DCS. Silas said this microscope would make her very jealous. Silas met some of the lab mice, and saw how they inject cancer cells into the mice. He is full of questions.

Over the years, with every tumor and craniotomy, Silas has made many donations to this research. He has contributed to the identification and, hopefully, treatment and cures of pediatric brain cancer.

Back to the hospital and chemotherapy. Silas is tuckered out.

Loving Silas

Sunday, November 23, 2014

Silas is puking his meds. He hasn't eaten or drank anything other than to take oral meds since Friday. The anti-nausea meds make him extremely sleepy, so this is how Silas is today. He's getting ready to take his oral chemo capsules, then 1 hour later, he'll have IV chemo over 90 minutes. Then he's done until tomorrow. His left arm is stiff, so I'm going to work it out and stretch it like OT does, and then I'll work on his left leg a bit. He has started calling this "MMNT," My Mom's Nagging Therapy.

He says he doesn't mind feeling "out of it," but he hates having everything come back up. I don't blame him. As he often does, he asks me to cuddle with him. Today, though, he tells me this is his gift to me.

Thank you all for your prayers. We'll be back at the bridge hospital tomorrow for sure, and will be there for Thanksgiving, in case any generous souls want to come visit us. HUGS to you all.

I know I've been asking for prayer for Silas a lot today and yesterday. I thought I should tell you about this morning. When I sat down to read my meditation and Bible, Silas asked me to sit at his feet and read to him. So, from page 170 in "Jesus Today," there were readings about Jesus watching over us, like a shepherd watching over his flock. After reading the Scripture nuggets, he wanted me to read the entire Psalm 62 aloud. We always discuss our reading, and we did so today, even though it was brief. We both liked verse 8: "Trust in Him at all times, you people; pour out your heart before Him; God is a refuge for us."

From Silas' heart to yours: Trust God.

Loving Silas

November 24, 2014

Silas is getting ready to go get a CT scan. He's had loose stools from the chemo. The nausea, vomiting, and head pain are unexplained. We are still at SLCH. Please pray Silas would get an appetite again, and be able to eat and drink. He also is scheduled to get a blood transfusion early this morning. He doesn't feel well at all.

Silas is not a complainer, ever. But he's letting us all know his head hurts and he feels pukey. He asks me to cuddle and hold him. I wish that made it all better.

Loving Silas

November 25, 2014

8 a.m. Yesterday and this morning, Silas' pain is so great he doesn't want any light, even with his eyes closed. He slept about 6 hours and woke up heaving phlegm. Neurosurgery was here to say the CT shows more brain bleed. They mentioned, and I am advocating for, doing an MRI to see exactly what's going on. Silas wants to be left alone. His sodium level is down, so they will address that, and give him a different drug by IV. I stretched out his left arm today, ignoring his objections, because we cannot let it get stiff. His left leg seems to be pretty flexible, even though he's been in bed 24/7. No loose stools in twenty-four hours. He will communicate a wee bit, and asked for me to read from my meditation book and Scripture — one of Silas' favorites, Isaiah 40:31. I remember the first time he asked me to sing that Scripture. I still sing it for Silas today and he loves it. Wait upon the Lord.

10:30 a.m. Neurosurgery was here. They want to do an MRI as soon as possible. The headache, nausea, and vomiting are not from the chemotherapy. I was pretty sure of that. He is receiving a loading dose of dexamethasone and increase in sodium before he goes to MRI, hoping to get his pain under control. Thank You, Lord, they work as a team here. Thank you, Silas' prayer team, for your faithfulness.

2:30 p.m. Silas Martin will go home to Decatur, Illinois, roughly the end of this week. St. Louis Children's Hospital is setting up hospice for him at home. Silas' tumor has grown quickly. This is what caused all the pressure, bleeding and fluid on his brain the past few days, along with the many symptoms. Steroids have been started to relieve the pressure, so less pain meds are needed. His doctors suggest he'll have a couple of good days before the steroids are not so effective, given the rate of growth of the tumor. There is nothing more they can do, except to make him comfortable and relieve the pain. Because the next couple of days will be his most alert and happy, Dad

Brock D. Martin and Shobi Martin and Nona Rosemary Martin are coming down tomorrow morning. I genuinely hope as many of you as possible will try to come visit Silas at home as soon as possible, so we have incredibly happy memories to store in our hearts.

When I discussed the situation with Silas, he told me immediately, "On this side or the other, Mom..." I broke down crying when I told him it looks like it will be the "other side." Then, we laughed and talked about how he will be able to walk and leap and dance for Jesus.

We discussed whether dogs get to go to heaven. Silas offered to let me know if Posh is there when he gets there. I told him I don't know anywhere in the Bible where it says he can do that. He smiled that beautiful half grin and asked wryly, "What, you don't want me to levitate some books?" My Silas.

I know I've said it many times, but I will say it here with more appreciation than you will ever know: Thank you–all of you–for your love and prayers and support.

Loving Silas

November 25, 2014

Friends starting posting on facebook:

"...Asking for prayers for my friend's son, Silas, and for their whole family. His brain tumor has come back and has grown so large that he is now being put on hospice.

We are in disbelief. We just saw this amazing young man on Friday and he seemed fine. Silas has never doubted Jesus through all of this, and he knows God is with him... he has the strongest faith of any 16-year-old boy I've ever seen."

"...Your son is such an inspiration~ and a Jesus warrior! GOD bless you ALL!"

"...Please continue Praying for God's Will & for Peace & Comfort. Silas is an AMAZING human being that shows God's love & awesome Faith. Such an inspiration & beautiful Soul. Thank-you for being YOU, Silas. You always know how to put a smile on anyone's face no matter the circumstances."

"...Hugs to you and amazing Silas who continues to show us the true meaning of being a Christian. Safe travels, and Our Redeemer Lutheran continues to pray for Silas and family. Love you!"

"Gloria, I asked our pastor to read Silas's favorite bible verse tonight at our Thanksgiving service... you two are so strong and I just admire you both..."

"With you, my friend........"

I decided to make one more post on my facebook timeline:

This is going to sound crazy, but here goes. If you know Silas, or have followed our posts over the past year, you know how Silas loves food, and loves to watch Man vs. Food. You know he loves to go to places where Adam Richman visited. When I asked him recently if there were anyone he wanted to meet in this world, he said, quickly, I might add, "Adam Richman!" This was right after we had finished reading the book, "America the Edible" by Adam himself. Silas loves for me to read aloud to him, because he is visually impaired. Until a week ago, he still could enjoy watching the Travel Channel or the Food Network. He even watched reruns of Man vs. Food. Here is my request: Please go to the facebook page of Adam Richman, and request that he come to meet Silas. Sooner rather than later. Someone around here has mentioned they have his e-mail address. Please share. Maybe if enough people contact him, Mr. Richman would honor Silas with a visit. Thanks, all!

Wally the Touch Dog on Loving Silas

November 27, 2014

From the facebook page of Wally the Touch Dog: "This is a hard post to write. One of the reasons that we loved our school visits is that we got to build relationships with the kids and watch them progress and grow up. I did not think we would have that at St. Louis Children's Hospital.

I was wrong.

Because we visit Oncology first (and sometimes only there) we see a lot of the same kids every week. We see them when they start treatment and watch as many lose their hair, get thinner, weaker and then, as they get through the treatment, we see the return to health.

But not always.

Today we found out that one of our very favorite kids has failed treatment and will be going home soon for hospice and end of life. He has fought long and hard but cancer is winning. Mom let me know that this was the small window of time that he was feeling better before the descent. I put Wally on the bed and he petted him for over half an hour. If you see his arm, he is wearing Wally's birthday wristband (given early). He looked better than I had seen him look in a month.

So, in honor of Wally's bacon-sneaking friend, please say a prayer for him, hug your children (human and animal), reach out to someone that you've drifted away from and remember that life is short and precious. Relish every moment."

God Loving Us

November 28, 2014

Silas gave out lots of hugs to teary-eyed nurses and doctors before being transported back to Decatur today. I cried as well. It was very difficult leaving St. Louis Children's Hospital. It has been our medical home for Silas since the middle of 2004. When it came to setting up Hospice, nothing went according to plan, or on time, but it all got done eventually. Silas is expecting several visitors tomorrow.

I cannot thank my friends and church family for their perfect timing and generosity as they have prepared our home for our arrival.

Silas can have visitors pretty much anytime. You may want to call first to be certain he's up to it. Thank you for your love and support, as always.

God Loving Us

November 29, 2014

There are things I know, things I know how to do, that I wish I didn't know as easily as I do. I successfully changed Silas' bag of IV fluids. I'm grateful it was uneventful. I wish I didn't know how to do this so easily.

I am still trying to unpack and organize everything here to make room for visitors. Silas will have a special group visit at 3pm this afternoon. I will keep posting pictures as we go along.

Silas' Martial Arts Instructor from years ago posted: "Silas Martin is officially a black belt now. His mother, father and brother were all in attendance. Some members of his dojo family were able to attend. Congratulations, Silas."

At the end of the day I wrote: I think this is what hospice is supposed to be about: making wonderful, fun memories, laughing with each other, telling stories on each other, sharing the joy of this moment, honoring the young man who has touched so many of our lives.

God Loving Us

November 30, 2014

Our sweet friend, Amy wrote: "Got to see Silas after church. That kid is amazing. Huge smile and thumbs up and a big hug. That boy amazes me. And worshipping this morning with Gloria Martin on praise team and watching Shobi Martin giving praise to God just left me speechless. Everything their family is going through and yet they continue to pour themselves out to God. Amazing family."

My friend, Phyllis helped us move Christmas. Here is her call to arms: "I pray that everyone had a wonderful Thanksgiving. I sure did. And now we are celebrating Christmas a little early this year. Our friend Gloria has brought Silas home from St. Louis and is under hospice care. We want to make sure he enjoys Christmas with has family and friends. We are having open house Christmas at Gloria's, Saturday, December 6th from 3-6 pm. All are welcome to celebrate with Silas... Now I need help making that happen. We need volunteers for many things. Yard clean up and outside decoration. Inside clean up and decorating, food and beverages for visitors etc. Bev is in charge of the outside work and will be starting Monday about 11am. Please contact her if you are willing and able to assist. If you are able to help with the inside things please contact me. I know we are all extra busy this time of year with our own 'stuff' but giving is what this season is all about. Let's show this young man our true hearts and come together for his last Christmas. Thank you!"

God Loving Us

December 1, 2014

Silas' friend, Blake, posted on facebook: "Amazing day today! Adam is a really cool guy. We even got to hear a few stories of his amazing food challenges and some cool people he's met over the years."

Yes, Silas' dream came true today. Adam Richman walked through our front door and straight into Silas' life. They talked about recipes from Adam's book that we'd read at the hospital, and about the history of bagels. Silas questioned Adam about the ingredients in the recipes he remembered. We laughed at the sometimes "adult" language I had to mask while reading his book to Silas. Adam lovingly talked about his own mother.

Silas' eyes never left Adam, except to take a brief nap. Silas actually got to meet his hero.

Donnie's Homespun treated everyone to lunch, which was Silas' goal all along.

God Loving Us

December 2, 2014

We called off visitors. No posting of pictures on facebook. Silas had a very special date. Our neighbors, Jen and Sara, had agreed to take on a monumental task. It was monumental in what it would mean to those Silas would leave behind. It was monumental in what it would mean to Silas, to bring some closure to his life while he could still communicate.

Because Silas was visually impaired, and now only had mobility on one side of his body, he was not comfortable writing things out. While everyone else left the house, Jen and Sara sat and talked with Silas. They jotted down what he talked about. Silas was not the most talkative person, so they prompted him to answer a few questions. What were his favorite memories? What were his hopes and wishes for those he loved?

Silas did not want to be videotaped so there was little of that. He was very self-conscious of his half smile. He had worked so hard in speech therapy to overcome the left side immobility. It took great effort to fight it in a conversation of any length. He didn't want to be remembered looking weak.

The notes they made that day were transcribed onto little yellow papers and folded. Each had an identifying name or note on the outside. They all went in a canister jar. On the outside was simply, "Silas' Memories & Wishes." The jar was given to our pastor to keep until after Silas was gone.

There are no words to adequately thank Sara and Jen for the gift they gave us by spending this time with Silas. It needed to be someone outside the immediate family. Not a one of us could have handled it. These beautiful women are so down-to-earth. I knew Silas loved and trusted them enough to be candid. I am eternally grateful.

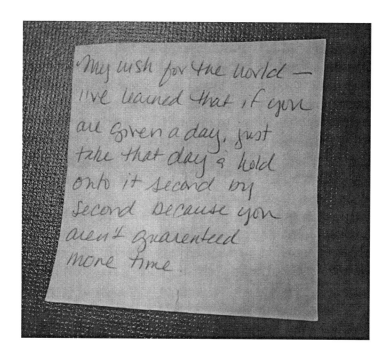

God Loving Us

December 4, 2014

Silas and I start out our day with a devotional, and telling each other something we are grateful for. He's not awake yet, so I'll tell all of you. I am so grateful for friends who are willing to do "whatever" we need right now. It's the little things I don't get time to do that drives me nuts. I am so grateful for Carla who is doing laundry for us, Sarah and Marissa who are doing dishes and general stuff for us, for Penny who calls and asks what I need at that moment, for Connie who is of little words but great faith in action, for Michelle who gave me a break so I could grab a bite to eat in the kitchen, for Sarah who read scripture to Silas in my place, and for many more who are too numerous to remember. The truth is, even when I am not okay, I still feel blessed and grateful.

Silas planned most of his celebration of life today. Pastors Steve and Scott were here visiting. Silas had selected the music for the service even before he left the hospital. He has chosen his pall bearers, and has only two more to actually ask.

We talked about playing the music from his iPad at the visitations. He has such eclectic taste. He hesitated, whispering to me, "Some of it is definitely not church-friendly."

Pastor Steve asked, "Did you listen to it?" Silas solemnly nodded. Steve went on, "Then it will be there to help us remember you."

Pastor Scott is Silas' youth pastor. He does not like pets. His wife and sons, however, love them. We have two cats, Angel and Ziggy. While Scott was at our house today, the cats kept jumping up on his lap. Scott pet them, tolerating them, smiling. Out of nowhere, Silas piped up, "Scott, when I'm gone, Angel is yours." We all laughed. Scott laughed the hardest. When the laughter died down, Silas spoke again, "Scott, after I die, Angel is your cat." We nervously chuckled a little more. Then Scott spoke incredulously, "Silas, you're serious!"

We all fell silent. This was a crucial moment. Scott finally spoke, "Silas, man, I love you... and if you mean this, I'll take her after you're gone."

Silas has plans only he can see.

God Loving Us

December 5, 2014

This has been a pretty good day for Silas, with less tummy troubles, and the perfect amount of guests. Silas has been so peaceful, even while picking out his own casket this evening. It is surreal, like picking out a new car from a catalog. Silas chose a beautiful "home" for his earthly body to be laid to rest in.

We've started looking forward to visits from our hospice nurse, Lisa. Silas loves that she brings treats for the dogs. I love that she assures me I'm doing everything I can for Silas. She is so attentive to details, and puts up with my never-ending line of questions. Some questions do not have answers, such as, "How long?"

"'For My thoughts are not your thoughts, Nor are your ways My ways,' declares the LORD. 'For as the heavens are higher than the earth, So are My ways higher than your ways And My thoughts than your thoughts...'" (Isaiah 55:8-9)

God Loving Us

December 6, 2014

We met as a family this morning, Silas included, with the funeral directors and the cemetery representative. We had to be sure Silas could have his last wish fulfilled, to donate his brain to Dr. Josh Rubin's research. Silas is included in all the decisions, which I think is amazingly brave for a 16-year-old. I also think this is something no 16-year-old should have to do. Praise God for good friends, and so much loving support holding us up.

It has been a bittersweet day. Today was our Christmas. Friends assembled earlier in the week to clean up the yard and decorate the outside of our house beautifully. Silas had lots of good visits, he stayed awake almost all the day, and he ate a little more than he has the past few days. We estimate over 300 persons came through our house to see Silas. There were even Christmas Carolers outside.

I was at Silas' bedside continually. With his poor vision, he often doesn't instantly recognize a person, and he has asked me to tell him who they are as they approach, or explain where we know them from.

People came from miles around, family, friends of Silas, friends of Shobi, friends of his Dad, and friends of mine. At one point, students from Decatur Christian School gathered around to sing "Bigger Than the Odds." There wasn't a dry eye in the house. Silas insisted on trying to hug the entire group.

I didn't see the kitchen or dining room during the festivities, but I know my friends manned the crock pots and dessert trays, washed dishes and made coffee, all day. When it all died down, it was especially sweet to see them spend time with Silas during the clean-up. Our amazing friend, Stephanie Gagnon, photographed beginning to end.

Many people brought gifts for Silas. He is already trying to decide how to "re-gift" them. He asked recently if he could bequeath all of his My Little Pony (MLP) figures and cards and paraphernalia to DOVE. DOVE is a domestic violence shelter here in Decatur, Illinois. He told me the MLP things speak of gentleness and joy, and he wants that for the children who have found a refuge there with their mothers. He also wants to contribute to the "Treasure Chest" at St. Louis Children's Hospital Hem Onc clinic. He has always said they need more items suitable for teenagers instead of babies.

Silas needed a nap during the afternoon. The people just kept coming. I greeted them over Silas. One young lady confidently approached, with gift in hand. She started talking to me as though she knew us well. I had no idea who she was. I don't remember if she had to tell me her identity or not, but I remember the moment I realized who she was, and both of our reactions. Our photographer even caught that moment. She was a friend of the family, one who always adored Silas. She and her family had been constant prayer warriors for over 10 years, from Silas' first battle with brain tumors. Silas and Maddy had often played together when our families were only blocks apart. And I hadn't recognized her, all grown up.

I can't help but think of the people who saw Jesus after He had arisen from the grave, and they didn't recognize Him. In Luke 24:13-35, it is clear they were kept from recognizing Him, until He broke bread with them. Can you imagine the look of amazement on their faces? John Chapter 20 describes Jesus' appearances to His beloved disciples, men who were more than friends. I try to put myself in their shoes, in an effort to understand the utter amazement of the truth standing before them. Those crazy women had been right. The tomb was actually empty. And to top it off, their Messiah had a brand new body! There aren't enough exclamation points to emphasize their joy and astonishment.

I cling to that utter astonishment we, too, have the promise of a resurrected new body. Silas looks to that moment without fear. Silas will have that new body soon.

"So, then, we are ever without fear, and though conscious that while we are in the body we are away from the Lord, (For we are walking by faith, not by seeing,) We are without fear, desiring to be free from the body, and to be with the Lord." (2 Corinthians 5:6-8)

God Loving Us

December 7, 2014

Friends, and friends we haven't met yet, continue to bless Silas.

Early this fall, an organization called "Wishes on Wheels" contacted me concerning giving Silas a Christmas "wish". Lots of gifts to get his mind off of cancer. I was so proud of Silas' response, "I really don't need stuff, Mom. Tell them to give the wish to another family who needs it." While relaying that message to the representative of W.O.W., I mentioned Silas had always wanted a sidecar ride. All the trips back and forth to St. Louis, seeing motorcycles, gave him the idea. Silas had decided it would be cool. She responded they would make it happen in Spring of 2015.

When they heard Silas had come home on hospice with little time to live, they called me. Today is the day they set to give Silas his sidecar ride.

This is a c-c-c-c-c-cold Sunday. WAND-TV and Herald & Review Newspaper coverage. This is amazing. Silas was interviewed by the media inside before I pushed his wheelchair outside. Once outside, we met over 80 motorcycles and riders waiting for him, whooping and hollering, in our alley. Silas was going to get his wish now!

In the TV interview right before going outside, Silas expressed his desire to give back to everyone who has given to him, and said, "I have a God who's bigger than the odds and I embrace every day he gives me. If you've been given today, appreciate it."

Silas' youth group visited tonight. The kids are having a hard time understanding, and difficulty saying good-bye. The youth pastor's wife, Sarah, posted in facebook:

"Coming home from Gloria's house tonight, I listened to my boys reading Bible verses from their new scripture wallets. What a beautiful gift! From the bottom of my heart, thank you, Silas."

Wishes on Wheels is a non-profit organization that grants wishes for children, located in Champaign, Illinois.

God Loving Us

December 8, 2014

Yesterday afternoon, out of nowhere, Silas suddenly said he wanted to donate his My Little Pony toys now. He declared they're all just gathering dust. He insists the children who have been victims of domestic violence could benefit, not only from a new "toy," but from the gentle message MLP promotes. I asked him to be sure, and he said yes.

Please pray these little symbols of "Friendship is Magic" will help the children who receive them, in the way Silas intended.

Silas keeps amazing me. I am so blessed.

God Loving Us

December 8, 2014

After a visit with Silas, a dear friend from church posted her thoughts: "So, just got home after a sweet visit with Gloria and Amazing Silas, and Brock. We took some dinner and... Lindsey and Colton sang a few songs for Silas. What a beautiful picture to see Silas trying so hard to sing along. I want you to know I'm having a difficult time finding words for this, and normally that's not an issue for me. Anyway, when they were ready to sing Amazing Grace, he wanted to be sure it was the Chris Tomlin version, My Chains Are Gone. Because his soon will be. Wow. What a faith. ... the Holy Spirit pouring through the worship and surrounding us with His Glory. And, in true Silas fashion, we had a good laugh. After the first couple songs I said to Silas, maybe they should take their act on the road. And his response was "or they could just come back here Friday and sing for my block". I asked if there was a block party planned? His response... "No, but there could be". I love that young man. May we all learn from him what courage and faith really look like. I am blessed to know him and his amazing family. His only prayer request as we were leaving? That it stay warm until the end. No snow. Jesus, please help this young man be free of pain and seizure, and may it stay warm in Decatur until he meets You face to face."

God Loving Us

December 9, 2014

Two weeks ago today, we were told Silas was being sent home. I sit here pondering how God has orchestrated everything, big and small.

The love and tireless efforts of friends enabled us to actually move Christmas. How many times in your life will you be able to experience that?

We found out Silas chose a hero worthy of admiring. Adam Richman flew out from his home in Brooklyn, New York, to fulfill a dying young man's wish to share a meal from a favorite establishment.

We chose a funeral director who allows us to have all visitation and celebration of life at our church, where we feel at home. In all of our dealings with them, we have been truly blessed.

A phone call this fall started the "movement" which culminated in so many bikers and supporters who gave Silas the sidecar ride of his life.

And now God is allowing Silas to have another desire fulfilled, and it is baffling me how all this worked together to make this one a reality.

Silas told me he doesn't want a hearse to carry him to the cemetery. Our funeral director offers a unique service, a glass trailer in which the casket is placed, drawn by a Harley Davidson. When the time comes, Silas' new family on wheels may escort him to his final resting place.

All of his life, I've known Silas was unique. I've seen how his gift for touching lives has grown over the past year. I am starting to see others know, too, as evidenced in these words from one of the teachers from DCS: "Hi Silas! Recently I heard you say in a news interview that you wished you had a gift for everyone that has given to you. I want you to know you have done this and more. How? Through the love, laughter, hugs, words of encouragement, just for giving of yourself and sharing God's love. You can rest assured you have given everyone more than they can ever give you. The legacy you are leaving in the hearts of those you have met and those you may never meet till they reach heaven. We are blessed to have known you in a personal way and we all love you so much. Thanks for giving something special that we will carry for a life time. The love of God has shown through every part of you. Love ya bunches Silas! You bring a big SMILE to my heart and all those around you. –Ms. Sandy"

God Loving Us

December 10, 2014

I was doing a load of laundry, and I smiled at something yet again Silas has taught me: all the clothing I need are the ones on my back, and maybe a week's worth total. He has always been so content.

"...for I have learned to be content whatever the circumstances." (Philippians 4:1)

The days since coming home have been filled with one visitor after another. We have a spiral notebook by the door for people to sign in and leave a message for us to read "someday." We've tried to take pictures of every visitor with Silas. He still gives the best hugs, even if they are one-armed.

Silas is well known for his love of food and furry friends. He has been blessed by lots of both the past few days. Silas loves to find that "sweet spot" each dog loves, as they cuddle with him on his hospital bed. I'm so glad we parked it right in the middle of the living room, where all the action is. As far as food, friends have brought horse-shoes from a restaurant in Springfield, Japanese soda pop from Fuji's, a giant sandwich called a "Shipwreck", and more.

Early in the month he could attack food with gusto. Now, the appetite is gone, but the love affair with food is not. He still makes requests with detail and a grin. Now he can't eat much.

Silas is on more and more medicine to prevent seizures, reduce brain swelling, and relieve pain. I set alarms for each one. I'm so afraid I'll forget one, and Silas will be hurting. I am so thankful we were allowed to maintain IV fluids for this entire time. I am certain this has played a big part in how well he's felt, how much he's been able to be awake. I am also thankful God has prepared me to monitor and administer Silas' meds and IVs. It is such an honor to care for him. All I care about doing right now is caring for Silas. I am blessed his dad comes each day, Shobi is home from college now, and I have amazing friends and church family holding me up through all of this.

God Loving Us

December 11, 2014

    I need to clear up some misunderstandings. Silas is on hospice. Some people think that means we have 24/7 care. That is the furthest thing from the truth. We have an amazing nurse who comes for about one half hour, one to two times weekly; an aide to help bathe Silas, one to two times weekly; a social worker and a chaplain at our calling if needed. I have the cell phone number for Silas' longtime hem onc doctor from St. Louis Children's Hospital. Silas has only a few, maybe two, weeks to live. His family needs some time alone with him. We have not had that privilege since he came home. It has been non-stop people wanting to visit. Don't get me wrong, we want Silas to have the opportunity to see the people who have always been important to him. We also want him to be able to thank the people who have supported him, either with continuous prayer, financially, or with support in any way. Silas has become a public figure very quickly, and it is exhausting all of us.

    I snapped at the family earlier, then burst into tears, all in front of Silas. Suddenly, his demeanor changed, and he started crying. I held him and asked him what was wrong. He finally spoke the words I've known all these years, "Mom, you know I can't stand to see you cry. It upsets me so much."

    I had crossed the line I never wanted to cross. Part of being Silas' mom was to cry in the shower, where Silas could not see or hear. I am still Silas' mom.

    We just learned a plan is in place to honor Silas with an annual charity motorcycle ride, *Spirit of Silas*. Silas himself chose the cause to benefit from the fundraising, Alex's Lemonade Stand Foundation. He is humbled by this act. Someone created a facebook page for the event, and plans are being made even now for next summer. It is odd to be planning memorials before he is gone.

    I am loving Silas living with cancer. God is loving us. God is loving us through this strange, unfamiliar territory. I am not Silas' mom remembering him losing a battle with cancer. I remember Silas living with cancer. I remember Silas living as only Silas did, adapting for his loss of vision in unique ways. I remember Silas giggling as he shocked people with his physical flexibility. I remember Silas' perseverance. I remember Silas defying the odds. Silas is still here. I still see all of that when I look at him. I am loving Silas living with cancer. And God is loving us.

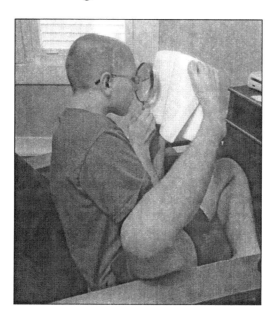

God Loving Us

December 12, 2014

Father, Lead me, because I can't do this alone. Silas is sleeping more and more each day. I can feel him slipping away. I know this is part of the process. I accept it. I don't have to like it. In many ways, this is all too familiar. You have allowed me to know for months Silas would not get his healing here on earth. You have allowed Silas to know as well. We didn't have to discuss it. You allowed this knowledge to coexist with our faith in You, God. You used it to grow our faith. You used it to grow our walk. You taught us to live intentionally, with urgency. And You have taught us to share that faith with any who would listen. I can thank You for all that, God. It's hard for me to thank You that my baby will be in Your arms soon instead of mine. But he never was mine, was he?

It's Friday. Silas woke with a "six out of ten" headache, so I administered morphine with his morning meds. This is the beginning of the end. We've had lots of visitors all day. Silas was most excited to see his favorite physical therapist. Becki helped us get Silas into his wheelchair, out to and in the car, all to fulfill yet another of Silas' desires. He wanted to visit a "real" meat market. This kid has been fascinated by TV shows about food, including those featuring meat processing and other strange yet interesting delicacies. Before today, we didn't even know we had a neighborhood meat market just blocks away. He wanted to see every cut of meat, but we arrived shortly before closing time. He shopped anyway, asking questions, and was all smiles. I think we all knew this was our last family outing together.

God Loving Us

Diana has been a friend of our family since the boys were toddlers. She captured what many have said about this blessed time together at home: "Hi Gloria, just sitting here thinking about you and Silas. Hope you are getting some much needed rest. I really enjoyed the visit with Silas, and still can't believe what an amazing young man he has grown to be. Job well done my dear! Melissa's nephews were in an auto accident last night that took the life of one of their friends. So as I told Silas, some are called home unexpectedly, and do not have time to say goodbye. I think he is blessed to have time to make the memories and express his love and faith. To you, Gloria, I give you my love and admiration, and my help whenever you should need it. God Bless."

December 13, 2014

Silas' pain is getting worse by the hour. He is having trouble staying awake. He has been sung to, prayed over, cooked for, hugged, kissed and loved even more today. He has asked so many unique questions, some serious, some totally off the wall & funny. He still has hope.

"Brothers and sisters, I do not consider myself yet to have taken hold of it. But one thing I do: Forgetting what is behind and straining toward what is ahead." (Philippians 3:13)

God Loving Us

December 14, 2014

Silas woke up with even more head pain. Meds didn't work efficiently, so we had to add more to the regular routine. The dimmest of light in the room made his head hurt even worse. I hung sheets over the curtains on the windows. It took two hours doing it by myself, but I got Silas bathed while keeping him warm. It's been a sweet time together, as everyone else is at church. He has slept most of the day. Not much interest in food, either. Please pray for less pain and no seizures as his time comes.

He silently mouthed the words to the praise and worship songs we sang around the front room this evening. Such a sweet time of worship. All of our days are numbered, right? Silas' days are getting shorter and shorter.

"My chains are gone
I've been set free
My God, my Savior has ransomed me
And like a flood His mercy reigns
Unending love, amazing grace"
(Amazing Grace My Chains Are Gone–Chris Tomlin)

God Loving Us

My friend, Erica posted December 15th: "Looking through your Facebook page...so many pictures, giving us a glimpse into the journey you and your family have been on these last few years. Silas has lived it so bravely, much more than anyone could expect of a boy his age. You have lived it with a Mothers fierceness... fighting, protecting, falling down, getting up... trying to keep all your plates spinning in the air, but knowing when to ask for help when you knew you couldn't do it alone. Through it all, you and Silas have taught us all lessons too numerous to measure, but I think "How to be a good Christian" undoubtedly tops the list! God certainly knew what He was doing when He sent Silas to you. I pray for calm and peace in the coming hours and days. Feel the prayers coming your way. Soon, Silas will be in the arms of our Lord, hearing Him say, "Well done, my good and faithful servant." Peace be with you, my friend."

God Loving Us

December 16, 2014–Tick...

Our Super Silas is in the "end stages." He hasn't opened his eyes but one time in the last 36 hours. He signed "I Love You" yesterday for the last time, and barely audibly spoke those words as well, although he couldn't hold himself up in bed. God only knows the time, but we are all around him right now, waiting for his sister to arrive from out of town. Thank you for respecting our privacy in these last precious hours. I removed his IV fluids today.

December 17, 2014–Tock...

Silas is still in "end stages" of leaving us and joining our Heavenly Father. Lisa explained Silas has a strong heart and strong body except for the cancer. It may take another day or so. Also, this doesn't take into account his strong will to live. He has always been a fighter. Please continue to pray the medications work to keep him seizure free. His pain is now under control. God bless you all for your continued prayers and support.

December 19, 2014–Tick...

Nobody knows for sure why Silas hasn't passed yet. Lisa spoke again of how strong his teenage body is. She also noted she can see his strong spirit in his face, even while he is semi-comatose. Silas is displaying all of the classic symptoms of a patient expected to transition in the next 4-6 hours, but he's had these symptoms for 36 hours, easy. Silas always has marched to the beat of his own drum, hasn't he?

I continue to medicate Silas to prevent seizures, reduce cranial pressure, and reduce body temperature. He has had high fevers day after day, 106° at one point. We continue to talk to Silas, pray over him, play worship music for him, and remind him Jesus loves him so much more than we ever could. I pray most importantly, for God's will. We all need to be reminded, some of us often, God is in charge. Period. I also pray, if it be God's will, He allow Silas to pass soon.

Lastly I pray everything we say and do glorify God. Silas would especially want that.

December 20, 2014—Tock…

Right now, it feels as though we are in a video and someone, somewhere, has hit the "pause" button for Silas. Life, such as it is, goes on around him, but we get no response. Lisa says again Silas has a strong, teenage body. He is able to hold on much longer than an aging patient.

I have spent so much of my life caring for Silas. I continue to do so, but it takes much less time. I took Silas' brace off his left arm, and it rests across his waist with his right arm now. He doesn't need to protect his immobile arm. He is on medication to reduce cranial pressure, and to prevent seizures. I have to set my alarms and stay on schedule, so Silas stays comfortable. His temperature is finally down below 100°, which it hasn't been for days. I am no longer rotating cool cloths on his forehead and armpits. He seems more peaceful.

It's time to do our devotionals. Silas never let a day go by without them, so I'm not stopping now. I believe he can hear me. I believe he can hear God's Word. I believe it is still sinking into his heart. I know for a fact how much it has affected my life as I read to him.

God Loving Us

December 20, 2014

My friend, Stacey, brought food over, and asked if she could sing to Silas. Mind you, Silas has been unresponsive, like in a coma, for almost a week. She explained to Silas she was going to sing a chorus they sing at her Grandma's church. This is one Silas did *not* know from his earthly experiences. He had never heard it. Stacey started singing.

Immediately, Silas was groaning—loudly—with her! His eyes never opened. He didn't speak words, but uttered different groans and sounds the entire time Stacey was singing. As soon as she stopped, Silas stopped.

Here are the words of that chorus. I think Silas was singing with Stacey. I believe Silas could see ahead. I believe Silas was seeing what they were singing about:

There's a light in the window And the table's set in splendor
Someone's standing by the open door
I can see a crystal river Oh I must be near forever
And I've never been this homesick before
Chorus:
See the bright light shine
It's just about hometime
I can see my Father standing at the door
This world has been a wilderness
I'm headed for deliverance
Lord, I've never been this homesick before

I can see the family gather–Sweet faces, there all familiar
But no one's old or feeble anymore (never grow old)
Oh this lonesome heart is cryin'–Think I'll spread my wings for flyin'
Lord, I've never felt this homesick before
(I've Never Been This Homesick Before: Writer Dottie Rambo)

Such a sweet memory–I clutch it to my heart.

I don't know about you, but I want to remain homesick while I'm here on earth. I pray I keep my eyes on Jesus, and on the glory ahead. I pray I can keep humming that chorus, and smile.

God Loving Us

I am up in the middle of the night to take Silas' temperature and to administer medications, then check facebook. I see so many posts of encouragement. God is so gracious and amazing. I am so certain He has a plan, a BIG plan, and we have had a small part in it.

Someone who knew Silas "B.C." (Before Cancer) shared this, "I have a beautiful memory of your sweet boy placing both his hands on either side of my face while he was telling me something that must have been important to him in the moment." That captures Silas' personality. If it was urgent to him, he found a way to get your attention.

I hope Silas has gotten your attention with the most important message he could ever deliver. He started saying a few months ago, "I am healed. This side or the other, I am healed." Silas wanted you to know you can have that same hope. Silas and I discussed only a few days ago that we will not give up praying for a miracle, and that God's miracle may not look like the miracle we want.

Silas bravely planned for the miracle of being able to see clearly, and to run into the arms of his Savior soon. He made plans for all of us who will be left here to remember him and celebrate his life in a few days. All the while, he would ask me questions starting with, "If I don't need a casket right now, can I (fill in the blank) next week?" He looked forward, asking to learn more about a local men's ministry, and buying meat at a local meat market for me to cook; all the while knowing the miracle of eternal life was a much bigger miracle than physical healing here on earth.

Silas' spirit is so strong, even now. His body is shutting down, and there is evidence the brain tumor is still growing rapidly, perhaps causing brain bleed. His spirit is so strong. His heart is so strong and full of love. He lingers with us still, unresponsive. Our biggest job right now is to keep him comfortable and pain-free.

I love Silas like crazy. I know Jesus loves him infinitely greater than I could ever imagine. I am ready for Silas to receive his miracle.

God Loving Us

December 21, 2014

We're all just waiting now. Silas is semi-comatose. He's down to skin and bones. He's had no food or fluid for about a week. I give him meds to prevent seizures and anxiety, and control pain, around the clock. It's like he's trapped in his body. Someone brings our family a meal about every other day. This helps. I truly want God's will. I hate seeing Silas like this. I only wish it was God's will to take Silas home. Today. I'm so selfish.

Silas was making such noises with each breath earlier. I read this is common in dying patients. I crawled up behind him and held him like he asked for during the last week or so before his body started shutting down. Such peace. Such an honor. Such heartbreak. I couldn't help but cry a little, even though Silas doesn't like for me to get upset in front of him.

Just now as I was praying, I realized I need to take Silas' advice today: "If God gave you today, appreciate it." I am going to make a gratitude list. I encourage you to join me.

God Loving Us

December 23, 2014

Silas left behind his wheel chair, his walker, his leg braces, his arm brace, his glasses and his white cane this morning, and ran straight into the arms of Jesus. He is now healed. He received his miracle. His chains are gone. I'm sure the angels rejoiced to receive Silas into Heaven. He has taught us so much about living by faith, about living in the moment.

I just returned from completing one of the first tasks Silas wanted me to do after he passed, take all of his "leftovers" and donate them to Northgate Veterinary Clinic. This included unused anti-seizure drugs, gloves, masks, and more. This was important to him that I do it right away, so I did.

As I neared our house as I returned, I saw that the florist had completed decorating the front of our home with dozens of colorful balloons. We want the world to know this is a celebration.

Silas is no longer trapped in his body, nor is his vision impaired. Silas is with Jesus. He wanted us to long to be with Jesus as well.

Celebrating Silas

December 27, 2015

There are nearly 400 signatures in the guest book from Silas' visitations and Celebration of Life Service. There was no funeral. It was a time of celebrating the life he led, the relationships he had, and the difference he made. There were tears, of course, as we started to mourn, but it was overwhelmingly a time of laughter, just as Silas wanted. Before Pastor Steve delivered a message of hope on Silas' behalf, three friends spoke publicly of Silas. One of them, Youth Pastor Scott Monette, certainly captured the essence of Silas with his address.

Eulogy

"Wikipedia defines *Brony* as "a name typically given to the male viewers and fans of the My Little Pony show or franchise. They typically do not give in to the hype that males aren't allowed to enjoy things that may be intended for females." I should know, since I have two little bronies of my own... and that's thanks in large part to Silas Martin.

My Little Pony was just one of the many ways Silas touched the people around him, and since it was such a frequent topic of conversation for him, I figured it was a good place for us to start as we celebrate the life of this remarkable young man. It's not surprising that Silas chose to be a fan of a TV show that most guys would write off as childish or girly, since Silas was not like most guys.

The middle school students in our youth ministry attend a conference every year in Indiana, and a weird tradition started years ago where the girls pain the guys' fingernails. The girls usually have to do a lot of convincing and even some bribery to get the guys to agree to it... but not with Silas. He was only too eager to get his nails done, and when the girls had finished with his fingernails, he put his feet upon the stool and had them do his toes, too. The other guys gave him a hard time when he got back to our room. Silas gave them a funny look and said, "I just spent the whole night in the girls' room. What did you guys do?" He may have liked a show that some think of as girly, but Silas wasn't girly; he was a ladies' man. When his family would talk to him about the marks that surgery might leave on his body, Silas would always say, "chicks dig scars." ...

I was recently given a copy of an autobiography that Silas wrote when he was 13, and it's so "him" that I have to read it for you today...

Although I am only 13 years old, I have had an interesting life. I was born at D.M.H. on August 3rd 1998, around five o'clock. When I was in the womb my head was turned sideways. When I came out I cried and cried. I weighed eight pounds, ten ounces. Mom named me after the Silas in the Bible, and my middle name is a family name. My first word was "gugguk"; I said "gugguk" for everything. If I heard a fire truck, I said "gugguk." I first started walking at seventeen months.

When I was two on Christmas I wore a Santa costume. The buttons on it were blue, yellow, and green. Once I got in my mom's purse and put lipstick all over my face. Sissy thought it was funny, and we have pictures of it at home.

On my third birthday I had a "Power Puff Girls" birthday cake. I had a piñata there at my birthday party full of candy, but it was hot that day so all the chocolate candy was pretty much melted. Later that year Shobi and I ate ants under a rock in the garden out back at that big white house in Warrensburg. That year I left the house in the middle of the night to go to my babysitter's house to watch "The Lion King". I remember I was jogging on the sidewalk to our house and I scraped my knee. I was a Preschool dropout at NWCC. I went to Macon Resources for speech, physical, and occupational therapies. We went to Disney World. I saw a Muppet ride I wanted to try, but we ended up doing a Star Wars ride. There was a fire hydrant that sprayed you with water if you got near it.

I rode the little bus to Warrensburg Lollipops Pre-Kindergarten when I was four. We walked to the library often. There were special locks at the tops of the doors in our house to keep me inside. Shobi and I worked together to unlock them. We ambushed Mom from the top of the bunk beds.

When I was five I wrote my "Ns" n reverse. I always got out of breath when counting to a hundred. I was diagnosed at five with brain tumors. These tumors had caused me to always feel hungry, messed up my sleep, caused me to have precocious puberty, and robbed me of some sight.

I started I.V. chemotherapy every week as I turned six. I went to my teacher's stables for a field trip and one of her horses thought I had a treat and nibbled on my hand. I went to Champaign once a week, St. Louis once every three months for an MRI, and many times for eye exams.

When I was seven I got my first F on my report card. I started oral chemo and I swallowed 16 pills at once every night.

At eight years old I got transferred to William Harris [public school]. I got bullied a bunch, practically every day it felt like.

At nine years old I got to got to the Springfield History Museum on a field trip. I still got bullied.

I was ten years old and started algebra, which I stink at. Again, I got bullied.

We still did a little more algebra when I was eleven. Yet again I got bullied. I got in a little bit of trouble when I spoke out about the earth not being four and a half billion years old.

At twelve years old I transferred back to Northwest. I learned about Minecraft. I died a lot in this game. Keith came over more often, I played Oblivion.

I had my thirteenth birthday at the Incredible Pizza Company. It was fun and I played on the bumper cars. I played laser tag and gave some points to my friend JJ, so he could get an eight ball. Mom bought, "The Sly Cooper Collection". Mom preordered Skyrim, and around twelve a.m. on 11/11/11 we went to GameStop and bought it. I had a weird dream about Skyrim.

Recently, Blake accidentally told me about a clip on YouTube called "I like trains." It's about an emo kid who says, "I like trains". Whenever he says it in the clip, an image of a train pops up and shoots by. As you can see, I've had a pretty interesting life so far."

[As you can see] Silas was odd and random; you never knew what little thing he would choose to remember for the rest of his life. Silas was also independent.

The first time I met Silas was at a youth group gathering. When I announced that we were going to play a game, Silas shouted, "a game!", threw his (white) cane down and sprinted down the hall. Now, I didn't know how much Silas could see; I only knew that I had a blind student who threw his cane to the ground and started running around the room. He was always leaving that cane behind, too–somebody would have to remind him not to forget it.

Silas was so independent that one Sunday, when his dad wasn't getting ready for church fast enough for him, he decided that he would just walk. So he grabbed his cane and his Bible, and he took off. Google Maps says that there are 2.6 miles between Silas' house and this church, and it didn't take him long to realize that walking was going to make him late. So Silas stuck out his thumb and hitched a ride from a total stranger. Silas always did things his own way.

So much so that nobody ever wanted to be the one to tell him that he couldn't do something.

A few years ago our youth group went to play miniature golf together. The group was pretty big that day, so we had to split up: half of us started on the golf course, and the other half headed for the go-kart track. Silas and I ended up in different groups, and I figured that one of the adults in his group would break the news that a legally blind kid wouldn't be allowed to drive a go-kart. When that didn't happen, I figured that surely they wouldn't sell him a ticket. When he came out of the clubhouse with a big goofy grin on this face, I just knew that the attendant at the track would see his white cane and send him to get his money back. Instead, the friendly attendant held his cane for him as he climbed into one of the karts. At that point I gave up on golf–I had to see this.

Silas drove as you might expect: erratically. He pin-balled from one side of the track to the other, and when he drove past the place where I was standing, he had a huge grin on his face. By this time, a crowd had gathered to watch Silas drive...and he didn't disappoint. It came time for the ride to end, and the attendant held up the sign that said one more lap. When Silas almost ran him over, I knew there was gonna be trouble. The next time around, all the other karts pulled in to the garage... but not Silas. He kept grinning from ear to ear as he blew by for another lap. The next time, the attendant stood in the track and pointed to the garage–and almost lost a foot. So he set up a wall of cones, but Silas ran them over like they weren't even there, dragging one behind him for half a lap. I was starting to think that Silas had to know what was going on by now, and that was confirmed when, the next time he came around, Silas finally drove his kart into the garage to avoid hitting the two guys who were standing in the track. He slowed down for a few seconds, then sped off through the garage, on to yet another lap. At that point, one attendant hopped in a kart and sped off to catch Silas. He clipped Silas' kart and spun him out, while the other guy shut off the power to his kart. They pushed him all the way back to the garage, and handed him his cane as he got out. When I apologized to them later, they told me, "Don't worry — it happens all the time." I highly doubt that. I've been doing youth ministry for 14 years, and I can tell you that a student like Silas does not "happen all the time."

Silas loved food. Nothing was too unusual for him to try, and he would often ask for things like Haggis or escargot when he was in the hospital. I was at Steak and Shake with Silas one night, and he had just seen an advertisement for the 7X7 Steakburger on the late-night menu: a huge burger with 7 patties of meat and 7 slices of cheese. The trouble was, it was only 6:00 when we were there, and the late night menu wouldn't be served for hours. Silas, of course, did things his own way: he spent the entire night hitting on the waitress and telling her how hot she was, to try and convince her to make an exception. He loved watching Man V. Food, and when Adam Richman came to visit him a few weeks ago, he asked all about the details of the recipes in Adam's book.

That was one of my favorite things about Silas: the questions he asked. He loved to ask questions and he expected answers. There was no such thing as an inappropriate question, or an inappropriate time [to ask]. Steve and I taught the High School Bible class at Northwest for two years together, and at least twice a week Silas would high-jack the entire class period with one of this questions. He wanted to know how things worked. And he wanted to know everything he could about God and about the Bible.

That's because, of all the words I could think of to describe Silas, faithful fit the best. Silas was faithful to his TV shows and video games, to his friends, to his family, and most of all, to his God.

159

In these last months, Silas became something of a local celebrity, and lots of people told him how strong and inspiring he was. But Silas would remind them that he wasn't the strong one... God was. Lots of people questioned why God would let this happen to him, but Silas never did. He was famous for telling people, "I'm healed, this side or the other." Silas asked me to bring the whole youth group over for a visit earlier this month. While they were there, Silas made sure to give every one of them a gift: a small wallet filled with passages of Scripture. He wanted us to know that God would comfort us in our grief. Silas left us too early, but he didn't leave us empty-handed: he left us with a legacy of faith that was richer and stronger than you would ever to expect to see in an oddball teenager who loved food and My Little Pony.

Music was a big part of Silas' life, especially this last year as be battled the cancer in his brain. One song in particular–Bigger Than the Odds–became a sort of theme song, and Silas wanted to be sure that everyone got the chance to hear and sing the amazing lyrics. With that in mind, let's continue to celebrate Silas' incredible life as we sing this song together."

My Tribute to Silas

There was only one song at Silas' Celebration of Life selected by someone other than Silas. I knew Silas as no one else could. I knew he lived his life as though he had no disabilities. I also knew he was aware of them, because we talked about them on a regular basis. Silas told me he never remembered being able to see well. This wasn't a thorn in his side. He never saw it as a cross to bear. He often joked about his vision impairment. I knew that when Silas breathed his last breath here and took his next breath with Jesus, his eyes were opened.

As the funeral director closed the casket, we rose to file out, to follow Silas to his broken body's final resting place. Immediately, we heard the joyous strains of a song written and recorded by Johnny Nash, *"I Can See Clearly Now."*

I can see clearly now the rain is gone.
I can see all obstacles in my way.
Gone are the dark clouds that had me blind.
It's gonna be a bright (bright)
bright (bright) sunshiny day.
It's gonna be a bright (bright)
bright (bright) sunshiny day.

Oh, yes I can make it now the pain is gone.
All of the bad feelings have disappeared.
Here is that rainbow I've been praying for.
It's gonna be a bright (bright)
bright (bright) sunshiny day.

(ooh...) Look all around, there's nothing but blue skies.
Look straight ahead, there's nothing but blue skies.

I can see clearly now the rain is gone.
I can see all obstacles in my way.
Here is that rainbow I've been praying for.
It's gonna be a bright (bright)

bright (bright) sunshiny day.
It's gonna be a bright (bright)
bright (bright) sunshiny day.
It's going to be a bright (bright)
bright (bright) sunshiny day.

Yeah, hey, it's gonna be a bright (bright) bright (bright) sunshiny day.

God Loving Us

December 28, 2014

During the last few months, for a devotional time, I would read to Silas. Normally, he would take a bookmark and randomly "find" a page to read in "JESUS TODAY". We would then explore one of the Scriptures there. I miss that time with him. He also liked for me to read my "sermon notes" I'd scribbled in the margins of my Bible.

Today, I was in Hebrews Chapter 12. I'm not the best at understanding or interpreting Scripture. As Shobi speaks of his studies at Lincoln Christian University, I realize more and more how little I actually know. However, I have some notes here in the first few verses, on "Letting Go" and on "running with endurance the 'race' that is set before us."

I have noted the "race" may be "the plan and purpose of God" set before us. I have to admit I don't want to finish this leg of the race this morning. I am dragging my feet. But I do have the desire to fulfill "the plan and purpose of God" he has for me. I trudge on.

I read to the end of the chapter, and, of course, found peace in the words of the last two verses: "...since we are receiving a kingdom which cannot be shaken, let us have grace, by which we may serve God acceptably with reverence and godly fear, For our God is a consuming fire."

My sermon notes summed up simply: "Be the Hands and Feet of Jesus." That's what we're going to do today, as we go on from here.

The best tribute we could pay to Silas is to Be the Hands & Feet of Jesus.

God Loving Us

It seems so strange to be able to walk out the door without making arrangements for someone to stay with Silas at home. It seems so strange to be able to take a nap. I took a much needed one this afternoon. It seems so strange to lie down to sleep at night without setting multiple alarms to administer Silas' medications. It is surreal to see pictures and video footage of the carriage carrying my son's casket to its resting place, and of the dozens of bikers who joined in "Remembering the Ride." It seemed so strange to do devotionals today without reading them aloud to Silas, so I decided to read them aloud anyway.

That small thing brought me comfort today. Singing worship songs at church also lightened my heart.

It all just seems strange.

God Loving Us

Today, I crossed several things off my list of things I promised Silas I would do, specifically for me, after he was gone. Honestly, I was a bit scared when I started, then I read this quote: *"When you're scared but you still do it anyway, that's BRAVE."* (Neil Gaiman)

I made phone calls to and appointments with all my doctors and my dentist. I had canceled all my appointments over the last few months due to my "relocation" to St. Louis area with Silas. My dentist even got me in this afternoon for my 6-month cleaning and checkup. I went back to my gym, re-enrolled in monthly membership, and talked to my trainer. This one was important to Silas, because he had seen how strong and healthy I had been getting, and how good I felt, when I was working out. Silas had been very proud of his gym-going mama.

I started gathering together some more of the things Silas wishes to donate to various parties. I talked to our Worship Leader, and I'm now back in the regular rotation to play the keyboard and be on vocals. I sat down and ate lunch, as I've been doing every day, whether I feel like it or not. I've been going to support group meetings, as I am doing this evening, and not only because I promised Silas I would. I go because I crave the fellowship I find "around the tables" and at Celebrate Recovery. I go because maintaining my sobriety is the only way I will truly get through this.

Yes, I was a bit scared when I started out today, but I prayed. I looked down and read a bit from the Bible I'd left open on the kitchen table. I did it anyway. I guess this made me BRAVE today.

God Loving Us

January 1, 2015

I'm thinking about God's perfect timing this morning.

I'm looking at pictures taken almost exactly a year ago. Silas was a little over halfway through his daily radiation treatments, so we snuck up to Decatur for the weekend. The pictures show how big Posh actually was and how Silas went about his activities with his 90-pound Great Dane on his lap. We lost Posh suddenly August 7th, shortly before Silas was diagnosed with the recurrent grade 4 tumor. She didn't suffer, and we didn't have to worry about a sick dog with osteosarcoma at home, while we were gone to St. Louis during Silas' last few months. Silas learned what it was to mourn then.

Now, I'm blown away how God timed Silas' passing at a time his brother, Shobi, could be home on break from college. We're leaning on our separate friends, shared friends, and on each other, during this intense awareness of the void in our lives. I'm so grateful I have the opportunity to continue the spiritual disciplines so deeply seated in me while caring for Silas. I can discuss my devotionals and readings with Shobi, who is learning so much about God and His Word in college.

Yet–and I say this with no regrets, simply observing–it took my child being in the hospital, terminally ill, for me to find the boldness to actually discuss *with my child* what I was reading daily, both in my Bible and in my devotional book. I became bold enough to talk about how God's Word applies to our lives on a daily basis. I became bold enough to share my personal struggles with the world, and to give glory to God for the victories He has provided.

I wish I had started earlier.

Dear Silas,

I want you to know your very last wish is happening right now. There is a team of researchers, doctors, and specialists who have assembled. They are working to make a difference in the world of brain cancer. I don't think any of us could have imagined the impact your donation will have. I am still trying to understand all Dr. Rubin and I discussed this afternoon.

You should know that there are others on the team besides Dr. Rubin who love you so much. Dr. King and Dr. Limbrick are there as well. At the first team meeting, the three of them made certain the entire team knew they weren't dealing with just any young man. They shared some of your antics, your jokes, your idiosyncrasies. Then they shared what an extraordinary person you were. I'm sure they chatted about your love of life, and how you just kept proving the medical community wrong time and again.

We know you had a rare type of brain cancer, but let me tell you why it was so rare. You had NF1, which you knew. Patients with NF1 often get brain tumors. Many of these tumors are gliomas, which you have had several in the past. Few are cancerous. Even fewer are aggressive. It is mind-bogglingly rare that you had a PNET tumor, of the worst variety. It was so aggressive it was trying to grow out of your brain! From the time of your surgery September 10, 2014 for removal of the recurrent PNET tumor, it was trying to take over your brain. Even as you went through chemotherapy to combat more growth, it was multiplying in size. I am looking at a printout of an MRI taken after you donated your brain to Dr. Rubin's research. It appears to me the tumor was roughly the size of my fist.

Part of what they are studying is using MRI scans in a much different way. Dr. Rubin was so kind to point out to me all the different shades of gray, bright spots, bright rings, dark spots, and more. All of this indicates you had several different "varieties" of tumor cells growing up there. They are going to be able to compare your "plain" brain cells to those in the tumor, factor in your genetics, and try to answer many questions. They will be looking at treatments, and what combinations of therapies might work on part of the tumor, but not on another, and figure out why. They are looking at the blood samples Daddy and Shobi and I donated, and using them, along with samples of your blood, to answer even more questions.

There are some very famous people on this team. (Other than you, I mean...)

I remember when Dr. King told you the tumor had recurred. You chose surgery and treatment afterwards. You always reasoned that, even if it didn't cure your cancer, the results of your decisions might someday help other children with brain cancer. I also remember your conviction when, faced with the possibility of not surviving the surgery, you said, "All I care about is donating my brain to Dr. Rubin." He finally has your brain, Silas. So much good is going to come from this.

I did ask some hard questions today, Silas. I asked Dr. Rubin to show me the parts of the brain affected by the tumor, and the functions of them. Now I know why you lost any mobility you had regained on your left side. Now I know why you might have struggled to communicate toward the end. Now I know why you fell asleep a week before you left us, never to open your eyes again. Now that I have seen the size of your tumor, I cannot imagine how much pain you were in. I am so thankful for hospice and the medications that kept you comfortable.

I promise you I will follow along, and watch over the research. I am so proud of you and your selfless attitude. I have heard people describe you as unique. After today, I realize there will never be a word strong enough to describe just how unique you were.

I love you always,
Mom

Work Cited

1. – (2011), *365 MOMENTS of PEACE for a WOMAN'S HEART–REFLECTIONS ON GOD'S GIFTS OF LOVE, HOPE, AND COMFORT*. Bloomington, Minnesota: Bethany House Publishers.
2. – Young, Sarah (2013). *Jesus Today: EXPERIENCE HOPE through HIS PRESENCE*. Nashville, Tennessee: Thomas Nelson Publishing.
3. – YouTube is a video-sharing website headquartered in San Bruno, California. The site allows users to upload, view, and share videos. Available content includes video clips, TV clips, music videos, and other content such as video blogging, short original videos, and educational videos.
4. (1961), Lewis, C.S. *A Grief Observed*. London, England: Faber and Faber Limited.
5. Wikipedia is a free encyclopedia, written collaboratively by the people who use it. It is a special type of website designed to make collaboration easy, called a wiki. Many people are constantly improving Wikipedia, making thousands of changes per hour.
6. (1975), *Twenty-Four Hours a Day*. Center City, MN: Hazeldon Foundation.
7. *The Bible:*
    GOD'S WORD Translation
    New International Version
    King James Version
    New Living Translation
    New King James Version
    New American Standard Bible
    The Message: The Bible in Contemporary Language